Arctic opening:
insecurity and opportunity

Christian Le Mière and Jeffrey Mazo

Arctic opening:
insecurity and opportunity

Christian Le Mière and Jeffrey Mazo

IISS The International Institute for Strategic Studies

The International Institute for Strategic Studies

Arundel House ⏐ 13–15 Arundel Street ⏐ Temple Place ⏐ London ⏐ WC2R 3DX ⏐ UK

First published December 2013 by **Routledge**
4 Park Square, Milton Park, Abingdon, Oxon, OX14 4RN

for **The International Institute for Strategic Studies**
Arundel House, 13–15 Arundel Street, Temple Place, London, WC2R 3DX, UK
www.iiss.org

Simultaneously published in the USA and Canada by **Routledge**
270 Madison Ave., New York, NY 10016

Routledge is an imprint of Taylor & Francis, an Informa Business

© 2013 The International Institute for Strategic Studies

DIRECTOR-GENERAL AND CHIEF EXECUTIVE Dr John Chipman
EDITOR Dr Nicholas Redman
ASSISTANT EDITOR Mona Moussavi
EDITORIAL Chris Raggett, Zoe Rutherford
COVER/PRODUCTION John Buck, Kelly Verity
COVER IMAGE iStockphoto/SeppFriedhuber

The International Institute for Strategic Studies is an independent centre for research, information and debate on the problems of conflict, however caused, that have, or potentially have, an important military content. The Council and Staff of the Institute are international and its membership is drawn from almost 100 countries. The Institute is independent and it alone decides what activities to conduct. It owes no allegiance to any government, any group of governments or any political or other organisation. The IISS stresses rigorous research with a forward-looking policy orientation and places particular emphasis on bringing new perspectives to the strategic debate.

The Institute's publications are designed to meet the needs of a wider audience than its own membership and are available on subscription, by mail order and in good bookshops. Further details at www.iiss.org.

Printed and bound in Great Britain by Bell & Bain Ltd, Thornliebank, Glasgow

British Library Cataloguing in Publication Data
A catalogue record for this book is available from the British Library

Library of Congress Cataloging in Publication Data

ADELPHI series
ISSN 1944-5571

ADELPHI 440
ISBN 978-1-138-77669-2

Contents

LIST OF ACRONYMS

AHDR	Arctic Human Development Report
AMAP	Arctic Monitoring and Assessment Programme
boe	barrels of oil equivalent
EEZ	exclusive economic zone
IPCC	Intergovernmental Panel on Climate Change
ISA	International Seabed Authority
LNG	liquefied natural gas
NEP	Northeast Passage
nm	nautical mile
NSR	Northern Sea Route
NWP	Northwest Passage
UNCLOS	United Nations Convention on the Law of the Sea

ACKNOWLEDGEMENTS

This *Adelphi* book is the culmination of two years of research, centred around the International Institute for Strategic Studies' Forum For Arctic Climate Change and Security, a joint endeavour of the Institute's Defence and Military Analysis Programme and Climate Change and Security Programme. We would like to thank the Swedish Ministry of Foreign Affairs and the Finnish ministries of foreign affairs and defence for providing the funding for a series of workshops on Arctic geo-economics, security co-operation and geopolitics in London, Brussels and Washington DC in 2012, a capstone seminar in Stockholm in 2013, and the production of this book. We would also like to thank the Canadian Department of Foreign Affairs, Trade and International Development and the Japan Foundation's Center for Global Partnership for supporting the Washington DC workshop.

More than 35 experts from 13 countries participated in the workshops and seminar, and their contributions were invaluable. Ed Hawkins reviewed the scientific content of Chapter One. Niklas Granholm, Bjorn Gunnarsson and Whitney Lackenbauer provided comments and discussion on our draft manuscript at a special session at the Global Strategic Review in Stockholm in September 2013. (Any errors in the book, of course, remain entirely our own.) Of our IISS colleagues, Sanjaya Baru, Sam Charap, Jens Wardenaer and especially Shiloh Fetzek made particular contributions to the success of the Arctic Forum workshops.

Finally, we would like to thank Nick Redman and Mona Moussavi for their thoughtful editing, and John Buck for his design skills. Just as physicians make the worst patients, editors make the worst authors, and we hope we haven't tasked their patience and humour too much in the course of producing this book.

As global warming makes the northern polar region increasingly accessible, two dominant and contrasting conceptual frameworks or narratives have begun to emerge. Many observers see the Arctic as a setting for state-based competition, even military confrontation, over territory, sovereignty and vast mineral resources. But this 'cold-war' or 'gold-rush' narrative is unrepresentative of the views of many parties that are already operating in the Arctic, such as merchant-vessel fleets, tour operators, energy companies, coastguards, militaries and diplomats from the Arctic states. Among them, the view is optimistic, but also somewhat cautious and restrained: optimistic about the potential economic opportunities to be found in the warming Arctic, while at the same time cautious about the many technological, environmental, human, political and climatic difficulties and uncertainties that would need to be overcome, and restrained in their approach to both opportunities and risks.

The first narrative is driven by events such as the 2007 Russian North Pole expedition, during which Arctic researcher and Duma member Artur Chilingarov planted a Russian flag made of titanium on the seabed at the pole, an act which many observers compared to imperial-era land grabs. A 2008

European Commission report identified the Arctic as a source of tension, 'with potential consequences for international stability and European security interests', and singled out the planting of the Russian flag as an illustration of this.[1] The Russians, however, compared Chilingarov's gesture to planting a flag on the Moon, manifestly not a territorial claim. The real purpose of the Russian expedition was to gather additional geological data to support their claim to an extended continental shelf (and its seabed resources), which they had submitted to the relevant United Nations body six years earlier. This claim may overlap potential claims by Canada and Denmark, which are yet to be submitted. That all three states are following established international law and agreed procedures is, in the second narrative, evidence that the Arctic is a zone of cooperation and consensus, and a model for dispute resolution for the rest of the planet.

The Arctic is certainly changing, and is doing so rapidly. There is no a priori reason to assume that this change will lead to conflict and confrontation, nor is there any reason to be complacent. This *Adelphi* book aims to provide readers with a sense of the growing geostrategic importance of the Arctic as a region and the wider, global influence it will garner through the effects of climate change. As seasonal sea ice retreats, the economic exploitation of the Arctic, via industries such as hydrocarbon extraction, fisheries and tourism, as well as the use of the region as a maritime thoroughfare for European–Asian trade, will transform the Arctic into an area of increasing activity. These changes are occurring as littoral states both cooperate more closely through multilateral forums such as the Arctic Council and compete more directly through military deployments in the region. At the same time, extra-regional states, particularly in Europe and Asia, are increasingly interested in the changes affecting the dynamics of the region.

This *Adelphi* provides a comprehensive overview of the physical changes occurring in the Arctic and the effects they are having, and will have, on regional and global economics, politics and strategy. The non-specialist reader is guided through the disputes, interactions, opportunities and challenges of the High North. The current state of scientific knowledge and projections with regard to the Arctic environment is assessed, as well as military and constabulary activity and territorial disputes in the region, both confrontational and collaborative; geopolitical effects on broader strategic relationships; and prospects for developing new formal and informal security architectures and governance structures for the Arctic.

The changing Arctic should be viewed as a sphere of potential cooperation rather than one of competition. There are potential economic benefits from international exploitation of the Arctic, although the riches are not as great as is often claimed. However, the region currently lacks the security architecture that would facilitate this cooperative dynamic. Any development of such an architecture will take place against a backdrop of rapid environmental change; accompanying changes in access and operating conditions; and shifts in the relationships between the five Arctic littoral states, the three Arctic non-littoral states and non-Arctic states that have interests in, or are affected by, the region. The military increases in the region that are currently occurring can largely be explained as Russia simply rejuvenating its decrepit Northern Fleet and Arctic littoral countries attempting to prevent the creation of a large ungoverned space. In the longer term, however, without a security architecture, any further militarisation could be viewed with suspicion by Arctic states.

What is the Arctic?

To the ancient Greeks, the Arctic was the 'region under the Bear' (*arktos*), and the Arctic Circle was defined by the motion of 'the Great Bear' (*Ursa Major*) in the night sky.[2] The modern definition of the Arctic Circle, in contrast, is 66°32'N, the latitude north of which the sun remains above the horizon for at least one full day in summer, and below the horizon for at least one full day in winter.

Using the Arctic Circle to define the boundary of this geographical region has the virtues of precision and familiarity, but in many contexts is arbitrary and obscures important differences. For example, the Arctic is defined in some scientific disciplines by the '10°C isotherm' – that is, the line north of which the average summer temperature (or the average temperature in July) is below 10°C. The region so defined coincides closely with the tundra biome, where low temperatures and short growing seasons prevent trees from growing, and less closely with the area of continuous permafrost. Sometimes such regions are referred to as the High Arctic, with the Arctic as a whole also including the subarctic, characterised by taiga or boreal forest. Other definitions are human-centred, based on the distribution of languages, cultures or peoples (all of which tend to broadly coincide with climatic or biogeographical regions) or even subnational political boundaries.[3]

The International Hydrographic Organization (IHO) defines the limits of oceans and seas in order to ensure consistency and continuity in official publications and notices, and in scientific reporting. The Arctic Ocean, as a body separate from the various seas north of the Arctic Circle, is limited to the waters surrounding the North Pole, for the most part well north of 70°N and in large areas north of 80°N (see Map 1).[4] Its adjoining seas include the Greenland Sea, between Greenland, Iceland and Spitsbergen, and – moving east – the Norwegian Sea, the Barents Sea (including the White and Pechora seas), the Kara Sea, the Laptev Sea, the East Siberian Sea, the Chukchi Sea (north of the Bering Strait between Russia and Alaska), the Beaufort Sea and the NWP. Another definition of Arctic waters based on temperature and salinity would exclude much of the Norwegian and Barents seas. The Greenland, Norwegian, White, Kara and Chukchi seas encompass some waters south of the Arctic Circle, while Baffin

Bay is entirely north of the circle but not adjacent to the Arctic Ocean. The Davis Strait between Baffin Island and Greenland is partly north of the Arctic Circle, while other waters often considered to be part of the Arctic – the Hudson Strait, Hudson Bay and the Bering Sea – lie entirely south of the circle. A very small part of the North Atlantic, between Iceland and Greenland, lies north of the circle.

For the most part, at the highest political level, the differences among the various definitions of the Arctic are moot, since those countries with Arctic territories under the more nebulous definitions tend to be the eight with territory north of the Arctic Circle: Norway, Sweden, Finland, Denmark (including Greenland), Russia, the United States, Canada and Iceland. Sweden and Finland do, however, lie entirely south of the 10°C isotherm. Moreover, the Arctic states are often grouped into the A5, or five coastal states, with territorial waters north of the Arctic Circle, and the A8, including the non-coastal states Sweden, Finland and Iceland. Iceland, however, does have a tiny territorial footprint in the Arctic: the small island of Grimsey, with 86 inhabitants, which straddles the Arctic Circle.

The various definitions of the Arctic are each appropriate to the context or discipline from which they derive, but for a work such as this one, which is of necessity and purpose interdisciplinary, a compromise is necessary. In the context of climate change, in particular, using definitions based on temperature or vegetation is particularly problematic. In 1997 the interdisciplinary Arctic Monitoring and Assessment Programme (AMAP), one of the five working groups of the Arctic Council (see pp. 39–40), defined its regional remit based on a compromise between the various definitions (see Map 2).[5] On land, following national preferences, the boundary lies at 60°N in North America, but extends south to about 53°N to include the Aleutian Islands. It follows the Arctic Circle through Scandinavia and Russia as far as the Urals (60°E), then meanders southeastwards through

Siberia to 60°N, at the neck of the Kamchatka Peninsula. At sea, it includes Hudson Bay and the White, Labrador and Bering seas, the last two of which lie entirely south of the Arctic Circle. In the North Atlantic it follows 62°N, but drops to 60°N to encompass the Faroe Islands (which are part of Denmark).

The Arctic Marine Shipping Assessment (AMSA), relying on national definitions of Arctic waters, uses yet another boundary for the Arctic maritime area.[6] The 2004 Arctic Human Development Report (AHDR) took the AMAP definition as a basis for practical reasons, with some minor modifications to conform to sub-national jurisdictional or administrative boundaries and the availability of data. Its Arctic comprises all of Alaska; Canada north of 60°N, plus northern Quebec and Labrador; all of Greenland, Iceland and the Faroe Islands; and the northernmost counties of Norway, Sweden and Finland. The Russian Arctic, where the definition departs from AMAP the most, includes the Murmansk region; the Nenets; Yamalo-Nenets; Taimyr and Chukotka autonomous districts; Vorkuta city in the Komi Republic; Norilsk and Igarka in Krasnoyarsky Krai; and parts of the Sakha Republic.[7]

This book adopts the AHDR definition for most purposes. Our focus is on politics, economics and other human interactions, so a broadly inclusive definition based on human factors is most appropriate. Moreover, the AHDR is an invaluable synthesis and source for a range of human activity in the Arctic. For the most part, however, we focus on a more restricted area north of the Arctic Circle, where warming will lead to the greatest strategic developments. Climate change will, to be sure, have significant effects on the more southerly parts of the AMAP or AHDR regions, and these will affect what happens in the High North and vice versa. But the Arctic is not physically, economically or strategically isolated from the rest of the world, and changes in the High North will likewise affect and be affected by developments far beyond the most expansive conception of the region. For example, there may be major changes to fisheries in parts of the North Atlantic encompassed by the AHDR boundary as the Arctic warms. But there may be similar disruptions to economic activity far from the Arctic as the High North becomes more open to maritime traffic and trade routes shift. In both cases, we will discuss the wider effects, but it is developments in the areas that have not yet seen significant human activity, and how those developments affect other regions, that concern us.

Moreover, for particular activities, especially shipping and maritime operations, an expansive definition obscures important sub-regional distinctions based on ice conditions and other factors that affect such activity.[8] It is thus important not only to bear in mind the various different definitions of the Arctic that may be used by the sources cited in this book, but also to be clear as to exactly what areas we are talking about in different contexts. For example, the proportion of the total Arctic population living in Russia ranges from 50–75% depending on which definition is used.

Geography and hydrography

The Arctic Ocean proper is divided into two deep basins, the Canadian and the Eurasian, separated by the submerged Lomonosov Ridge, which runs from the Laptev Sea to Ellesmere Island, crossing the North Pole. The Eurasian Basin reaches a depth of 4,200 metres and is further divided by the Gakkel Ridge into the Amundsen and Nansen basins. It is bounded to the south by Greenland, the Svalbard archipelago and Russia's Taimyr Peninsula. The shallow continental shelf underlying the Barents, Kara, Laptev, East Siberian and Chuckchi seas extends up to 1,000 kilometres or more from the Russian coast. The Canadian Basin reaches depths of 3,500 metres and is also divided into sub-basins by the Alpha Ridge. Except in the Beaufort Sea, the continental shelf extends only 50–100km off the North American coastline. Warm currents flow into the Arctic through the shallow and narrow Bering Strait, the deep Fram Strait between Greenland and Svalbard, and the Barents Sea; these currents contribute to the relative accessibility of the Norwegian and Barents seas compared to the rest of the Arctic. Cold currents leave the Arctic through the Fram Strait and the Canadian Archipelago; at least three-quarters of the water exchange in either direction flows through the Fram Strait. The distribution of sea ice is affected by temperature, winds and currents; the main ice-circulation systems are the clockwise Beaufort Gyre in the Canadian Basin, in which ice can circulate for more than five years, and the Transpolar Drift, which takes two to four years to transport ice from the East Siberian and Laptev seas through the Fram Strait.[9]

The Arctic land area, as defined by AMAP, comprises about 13.4 million km²: 5.5m km² in Russia, 4m km² in Canada, 1.4m km² in Alaska, 2.2m km² in Greenland, and the remainder split about evenly between Iceland, the Faroe Islands and Svalbard on the one hand, and continental Scandinavia on the other.[10] About 2m km² is covered by mountain glaciers and ice caps, and the Greenland Ice Sheet.[11] Most of the area is underlain by permafrost to varying depths. Most precipitation in the region falls as snow, resulting in rapid melting and run-off in the spring. Much of the ice-free land is unvegetated, and most of the remainder is characterised by tundra or poorly drained wetland.

A moving target

The Arctic is undergoing rapid change, both physically and politically, with the political change driven by the physical. In the last ten years, there have been comprehensive assessments of human development, the economy, maritime and shipping activity, climate change, pollution, ecosystems and hydrocarbons in the Arctic, among other factors. Such assessments draw on available data from scientific literature, as well as from the eight Arctic nations and any number of sub-national political divisions. The quality of the data varies from subject to subject and from region to region, and is not always timely. Given the pace of change, such assessment reports can often be obsolete, in part, even before they are published. It is often better, therefore, to rely on them as snapshots of conditions at a particular time, even if the conclusions must be tempered by more recent data or trends in some areas when comparable data for other regions is not available.

This is, of course, a perennial problem for analysts, but it is particularly acute with regard to the Arctic, both in terms of the rate of change and the availability of information. It is especially problematic with regard to projections of climate change, which are constantly being improved and refined, and for energy and mineral reserves and other economic activity. The most recent comprehensive report on the economy of the Arctic, for example, was published in 2009, and most of the data predates the global financial crisis and economic downturn. Similarly, the revolution in unconventional hydrocarbons, a phenomenon which is still occurring, has altered the playing field for Arctic oil and gas. Politically, too, the Arctic is in a state of flux, with ongoing bilateral and international negotiations on a range of issues, and new agreements, forums, strategy documents and commercial consortia emerging every year.

While these issues must be borne in mind, this *Adelphi* focuses on strategic trends over the medium term rather than on short-term developments, interesting though they may be. Confident predictions can be made on the direction of some of those strategic trends, particularly the effects of climate change, even if specific forecasts are impossible. This, in turn, suggests that increased human activity – in extractive resources, tourism, maritime industries, and military and paramilitary deployments – is likely. It is impossible to accurately predict how much of the Arctic will be navigable and for what period of time; which resources can and will be extracted; or which military assets will be moved northwards. Nevertheless, it is possible to say that the Arctic's geostrategic importance is increasing. The issues of the Arctic, as reflected in the burgeoning membership of the Arctic Council, are no longer confined to the High North but affect the whole world.

Notes

1   'The European Union and the Arctic Region', European Commission, 20 November 2008, http://eur-lex. europa.eu/LexUriServ/LexUriServ. do?uri=COM:2008:0763:FIN:EN:HT ML.

2   Henry George Liddell and Robert Scott (eds), *A Greek–English Lexicon* (Oxford: Oxford University Press, 1940), http://www.perseus.tufts. edu/hopper/text;jsessionid=84 DB0092238741D9E90B32ECFC 9C67EB?doc=Perseus%3atext %3a1999.04.0057, 'Arktikos'.

3   See Oran R. Young and Niels Einarsson, 'Introduction: Human Development in the Arctic', in *Arctic Human Development Report* (Akureyri: Stefansson Arctic Institute, 2004), pp. 17–18; Conservation of Arctic Flora and Fauna Working Group, Arctic Council, *Arctic Flora and Fauna* (Helsinki: CAFF, 2001), pp. 11–13.

4   International Hydrographic Organization, *Limits of Oceans and Seas* (Monte Carlo: IHO, 1953).

5   AMAP, *Arctic Pollution Issues* (Oslo: AMAP, 1997), pp. 6–7.

6   US Arctic Research Commission, *Arctic Marine Shipping Assessment 2009* (Akureyri: PAME, 2009), p. 17.

7   Young and Einarsson, 'Introduction: Human Development in the Arctic', in *Arctic Human Development Report*, pp. 17–18.

8   Willy Østreng et al., *Shipping in Arctic Waters: A Comparison of the Northeast, Northwest and Trans Polar Passages* (New York: Springer, 2013), pp. 3–5.

9   For more detailed descriptions of Arctic bathymetry and hydrography, see AMAP, *Arctic Pollution Issues*, pp. 20–23; US Arctic Research Commission, *Arctic Marine Shipping Assessment 2009*, pp. 16–23; and Navy Environmental Prediction Research Facility, 'Forecasters Handbook for the Arctic', http://www.nrlmry.navy. mil/forecaster_handbooks/Arctic/ Forecasters%20Handbook%20 for%20the%20Arctic.02.pdf.

10 AMAP, *Arctic Pollution Issues*, pp. 13–14.

11 AMAP, *Arctic Climate Impact Assessment* (Cambridge: Cambridge University Press, 2005), p. 202.

CHAPTER ONE

The warming Arctic: contexts

From a global perspective, the Arctic has been a geographical, cultural and imaginal periphery, and as it becomes more mainstream this legacy informs a range of sometimes overlapping, sometimes conflicting visions and mindsets with regard to the region. It is many things to many people: a homeland; a terra incognita; a magnet for cultural emissaries and tourists; a storehouse for resources; an environmental linchpin and bellwether; a scientific laboratory; and a theatre for military operations.[1] To understand the strategic implications of a changing Arctic, whether economic, political or military, it is necessary to first understand both the starting conditions – the current state of the Arctic – and how the regional environment is expected to change. This chapter briefly reviews the human and environmental history of the Arctic; examines scientific projections for the region's climate in the context of global warming; surveys current demographics and economic activity; and discusses the legal frameworks and international forums relevant to the region and the national Arctic strategies of interested states.

Historical background

The modern indigenous populations of the Arctic descend from hunter-gatherers who migrated north as the ice sheets retreated at the end of the last ice age, or moved eastwards from Siberia and Alaska to Greenland. The modern peoples of the High Arctic in the Americas, known collectively as Inuit,[2] descend from the most recent wave, which spread from Alaska as far as Greenland about 1,000 years ago.[3] Parts of the Arctic were integrated into the European economy as early as the ninth century. The Viking expansion out of Norway settled Iceland in the ninth and tenth centuries, and southwest Greenland soon thereafter, although the Greenland colonies died out in the fifteenth century as climatic conditions worsened. In the ninth century, a Norwegian Viking trader named Ottarr, who lived somewhere near modern-day Tromsø, 250km north of the Arctic Circle, described to the English King Alfred the Great a voyage he had undertaken around the top of Norway and into the White Sea. He hunted whale and walruses, and traded with the indigenous population for ivory and furs. It is likely that he was following an established trade route. His own wealth derived from trade and reindeer husbandry, probably conducted by indigenous peoples whom he ruled.[4] Commercial cod fisheries were set up in Arctic waters to supply the European market around this time.[5]

European interest in the Arctic increased significantly in the sixteenth century, after the discovery of the New World and the sea route around the Cape of Good Hope into the Indian Ocean, as part of a broader search for alternative trade routes to China and the East Indies. British and Dutch explorers, mostly financed by commercial interests, probed the edges of the Canadian Archipelago in search of the Northwest Passage (NWP), discovering Hudson Bay and reaching 78°N. The discovery of Spitsbergen by Dutchman Willem Barentsz in 1596 while searching for a Northeast Passage (NEP) around Siberia (one of his voyages included seven merchant ships carrying goods intended for the Chinese market) led to the rise of an extensive whale fishery around Spitsbergen, later expanded into

Greenland waters. For several decades in the early seventeenth century, there was sporadic fighting between whalers and even warships from England, Holland, France and Denmark, as well as between fleets from different English ports, over access to the fisheries, and to ports and other land-based facilities in this part of the Arctic.

The impetus for the exploration of Arctic routes to Asia waned after Portugal lost its monopoly over the southern route around Africa in the seventeenth century. But the Russians continued to explore the northern seas as part of the fur trade; in the sixteenth century, trade between the Kara and White seas amounted to several thousand tonnes of goods per year.[6] By the mid-seventeenth century, Russian vessels had navigated most of the Northern Sea Route (NSR) from the White Sea to the Bering Strait, albeit never in one continuous voyage. Organised, state-sponsored expeditions in the eighteenth century led to the discovery of Alaska and the extension of the Russian fur trade down the coast of North America, as far south as California. (The United States purchased Alaska from Russia in 1867 for US$7.2 million.)

Organised exploration of the Arctic received a significant boost after the end of the Napoleonic wars in 1815, when the British Admiralty under John Barrow used surplus warships and unemployed officers to conduct a broad programme of geographical and hydrographical investigation, much of it focused on the High North.[7] These efforts produced a legacy of British interest in Arctic exploration and science: the United Kingdom currently produces more Arctic research than any other non-Arctic state, both in absolute terms and as a percentage of its overall research effort.[8] The Admiralty's programme also sparked a revolution in cultural perceptions and imaginings of the polar regions that persists, in the UK and elsewhere, to this day.[9] This period of exploration continued approximately until the First World War: the first continuous transits of the Northeast and Northwest passages took place in 1878 and 1906; the North Pole was reached in 1909 and the South Pole two years later.

As the 'golden age' of polar exploration was ending, a new age of commercial and industrial activity was beginning. Although iron had been mined in Arctic Sweden from the middle of the eighteenth century, for example, the completion of a railway to Gällivare in 1888 opened the country's Arctic regions to a resource rush: ores, timber and hydropower fuelled Sweden's industrialisation. This first Arctic railway was extended to Kiruna, which produces most of Europe's iron, in 1899, and to the purpose-built ice-free port of Narvik in Arctic Norway in 1902. Coal mining began on Spitsbergen in 1899; gold mining began in Alaska and the Yukon in the 1880s; and cryolite, at one time important for aluminium processing and other uses, was mined in Ivittuut in Greenland on an industrial scale from the mid-nineteenth century. A railway was extended to the Finnish Arctic in 1909, and the ice-free Russian port of Murmansk, with a rail connection to the south, was established in 1915. That same year, the first permanent radio station above the Arctic Circle was established on Dikson Island in the Kara Sea, followed in quick succession by three more. The first flight of a fixed-wing aircraft north of the Arctic Circle, by a Russian army pilot, took place in August 1914.[10]

As economic activity in the Arctic increased, the region also grew in military-strategic importance. This new focus was most evident beginning with the Second World War (see Chapter Four), while during the Cold War the use of submarines under the Arctic ice clearly reflected the now-entrenched military-strategic importance of the region. This was exemplified by the fact that Moscow viewed the Arctic as a safe transit route that could service much of the country. The Russians therefore continued to build up navigational infrastructure along the NSR. Annual traffic on the route exceeded 1m tonnes in 1961, peaked at over 6.5m tonnes in 1987 and fell to 1.5m tonnes (the lowest level since 1965) in 1998. Since then, it has made a modest recovery, to the levels of the late 1960s. The vast majority of this traffic was between ports along the route rather than transits.[11]

This is, to be sure, only a quick and limited survey of Arctic history, omitting much detail. This chapter later presents a snapshot survey of the present state of human activity in the region. Together, these provide the general context in which to assess potential strategic developments as global warming makes the Arctic increasingly accessible.

The changing climate

The Arctic is clearly warming, and has been since the middle of the nineteenth century.[12] The most visible and immediately consequential effect of this is a decline in the area of the Arctic Ocean covered by ice year round (see p. 24). This downward trend has accelerated since the turn of the millennium.[13] This is only part of the story, however: seasonal land snow cover and ice cover on lakes and rivers are also declining; permafrost is thawing; and mountain glaciers and ice caps, and the Greenland Ice Sheet are melting. But these trends need to be considered against the backdrop of long-term patterns of change in the Arctic climate. In terms of the economic, political, social and strategic consequences, it does not really matter if a warming trend is natural or due to human activity, but it does appear that higher temperatures and declining ice over the last 150 years or so are anomalous in comparison to historical variability.[14]

For the last 2.5m years, the Earth has been experiencing an ice age, characterised by cyclic cold, glacial periods and warmer 'interglacials'. Over the last 700,000 years, glacial periods have tended to last about 100,000 years, separated by brief interglacials when conditions were close to those of the present day. (Technically, the Ice Age has not ended; we are just in another interglacial, or would be, in the absence of human-induced global warming.) In the last major warm period, between 120,000 and 130,000 years ago, Arctic summer temperatures were 5°C higher than at present, and sea levels were about five metres higher, due to loss of glaciers and much of the Greenland Ice Sheet. The most recent glacial period peaked about 21,000 years ago, with annual temperatures in the Arctic some 20°C colder than at present. The current warm period began 16,000 years ago, and

Measuring sea ice: extent, area, volume, age and thickness[15]

Scientists measure Arctic ice by dividing the region according to a grid pattern; for example, the US National Snow and Ice Data Center (NSIDC) uses nominal 25×25km grid squares. There is a continuous satellite data record of sea ice beginning in 1979; before then, the data, including ship observations of the sea-ice edge, are more patchy, and before 1900 mostly based on proxies. A grid square is considered **ice-free** if less than an arbitrary proportion of it (usually 15%) is covered with ice. **Sea-ice extent** is defined as the total area of the grid squares with an ice concentration higher than this threshold. Thus, a 625km^2 cell with anywhere from 15–100% ice concentration adds 625km^2 to the total sea-ice extent. **Sea-ice area** takes into account the varying concentration in individual grid cells, so that a 625km^2 cell with 15% ice concentration adds only 93.75km^2 to the total area covered.

A more meaningful metric, however, is **sea-ice volume**. If sea-ice area remains constant but the ice becomes, on average, thinner, the total amount of ice will decline. The thickness of the ice is related to its age: new ice forms in winter underneath **multi-year ice**, or ice that has survived at least one summer melt season. **First-year ice** – ice that has formed over the course of the winter in ice-free water – is thinner, making it more likely to melt in subsequent summers and easier for icebreakers to navigate. Thus, although the extent and area of winter sea ice is much less sensitive to warming trends than is summer sea ice, changes in the percentage and average age of multi-year ice mean that the winter sea-ice volume can be affected much more rapidly. Finally, the amount of melt in the summer is affected by the timing of the melt season, as well as by the thickness of the ice. Sea ice peaks in March and is at a minimum in September.

Because it takes several decades' worth of data to distinguish climate trends from year-to-year variations in weather, annual or decadal ice data are often presented not in absolute numbers but in terms of the anomaly they represent compared to a baseline, such as the average value for the period 1979–2000. (In July 2013, the NSIDC changed its baseline from 1979–2000 to 1981–2010, to match the World Meteorological Organization standard.)

although warming proceeded in fits and starts, the trend was firmly established by 12,000 years ago – the traditional end of the Ice Age – and by 6,000 years ago sea levels and ice volumes were close to current conditions.[16]

The temperature story is reflected in the sea ice: year-round ice developed in the Arctic Ocean as early as 13m–14m years ago, although its extent and duration varied. The ocean may have been seasonally ice-free during particularly warm interglacials before 3m years ago, and there were especially mild ice conditions 130,000, 75,000 and 10,000 years ago.[17] This periodic warming ultimately stemmed from increased solar radiation in the Northern Hemisphere, due to cyclical variations in the Earth's orbit and axis, and levels peaked 11,000 years ago, when summer temperatures in the Arctic were 1–3°C above twentieth-century averages. From then until about the time of the Industrial Revolution, there was a general cooling trend in the region.[18]

Human-induced global warming has reversed this trend. Since the second half of the nineteenth century, the global average surface temperature has increased by 0.78°C, with the rate of warming over the last six decades more than three times that of the preceding five.[19] It is extremely likely that most of this recent warming is due to increased greenhouse-gas concentrations in the atmosphere caused by human activity.[20] The rate of warming in the Arctic is approximately twice as high as the global average, and is particularly rapid in the interior parts of northern Asia and northwestern North America, north of 60°N.[21] From 1953–2006, the minimum annual Arctic sea-ice extent declined by an average of 7.8% per decade. This decline was not uniform due to natural variability but did accelerate in the second half of the period.[22]

Since 2005, temperatures at most locations in the Arctic have been higher than at any time in the historical record, with average annual temperatures consistently about 1.5°C above 1961–90 levels. Temperatures over the Arctic Ocean in autumn and early winter in the first decade of the twenty-first century were more than 4°C warmer than during the second half of the twentieth century, the fastest rate of warming for any season or region on the planet.[23] The average Arctic temperature is now higher than at any time in the last 2,000 years, while ice extent and volume are at record lows.[24]

These trends are illustrated by Figures 1.1–1.4. Figure 1.1 shows the changes in summer temperatures in the Arctic over the last 2,000 years in relation to the average for 1961–90. The long-term trend is downward, from a starting point somewhat cooler than in the late twentieth century. Within that trend, decade-scale fluctuations are evident, but the upturn after the middle of the twentieth century is dramatic and clearly exceeds the fluctuations of the preceding two millennia. Figure 1.2 shows the sea-ice extent over the course of the year for 2013 compared to the years with the two lowest minima – 2012 and 2007 – and the average for 1979–2000. The large loss of summer ice and the more modest decline in winter ice are evident. Figure 1.3 shows the minimum area covered by ice during the record-low month of September 2012, compared to the 1979–2000 median. Finally, Figure 1.4 shows the decline in total Arctic ice volume for both the winter maximum (April) and the summer minimum (September) since 1979. Although the decline is still more marked in summer than in winter, the difference is much less, compared to the decline in ice extent. This is due to the overall thinning of the ice and the decline in multi-year ice. Most notable, however, is that the annual maximum ice volume in April is now nearly at the level of the September minimum for 1979. In other words, the amount of ice in the Arctic in winter is approaching the levels that were found during the summer only 35 years ago.

This warming and loss of ice is projected to continue. In 2007 the Intergovernmental Panel on Climate Change (IPCC) reported that mean annual warming in the Arctic in climate-model simulations was double the Earth's warming as a whole, and over four times as great in winter. The warming was expected to be 3.4–5.9°C by the end of the century, depending on emissions scenarios, but with a wide range of uncertainty (plus or minus about 50%) between different models.[25] The IPCC models projected the minimum summer ice coverage by 2080–2100 to be 2.3m–3.3m km², or 46–60% less than the baseline of 5.6m km² in 1979–99.[26] But these warming projections proved woefully conservative. In more recent years, the ice decline has been much more rapid, with the record 2012 minimum at 3.41m km².[27] Even at the time, it was clear that the models were too conservative, underestimating the changes that were actually taking place and running about 30 years behind the observed trend.[28]

Using a subset of the IPCC models selected according to how well they had performed up to that point, one team of scientists projected a nearly ice-free Arctic Ocean for at least part of the summer by 2037, with half of the model projections falling between 2028 and 2046.[29] ('Nearly ice-free' is defined as less than 1m km² ice cover; some ice is expected to linger in restricted areas for much longer but would be of little significance.) Three years later, they updated their work with more recent data and new models devised for the next IPCC Assessment Report, due to appear at the end of 2013. They reported 2035 as an expected date for a nearly ice-free Arctic Ocean in the summer, with all models falling within the range of 2021–43.[30] Two other methods used to project Arctic sea ice are extrapolation of the observed trends, especially in sea-ice volume; and the probabilistic argument that, as the decline in sea ice is not steady but subject to fluctuations based on natural processes, several more individual years involving dramatic loss of ice, as occurred in 2007 and 2012, will be needed before the Arctic is nearly ice-free in summer. The projected timings from these three approaches are around 2020 from extrapolation, 2030 from the probabilistic approach and 2040 from the models.[31] In 2010 the International Institute for Strategic Studies (IISS) reported that the expert consensus view was that there could be some seasonally ice-free years by 2040–60; the consensus now seems to centre around a date several decades earlier.[32] There is still a great deal of uncertainty, but it is clear that conditions in the Arctic are changing more rapidly than was expected only a few years ago.[33]

This holds true for impacts beyond the sea ice as well. Surface temperatures are now projected to rise by 3–6°C by 2080 (6–7°C in areas of sea-ice loss and 2–3°C over land), although this is subject to the usual uncertainties in modelling a dynamic climate system. Overall, precipitation will increase, but some areas will become drier due to increased evaporation and changes in drainage as permafrost melts. The duration of snow cover is projected to decrease by 10–20% over most of the region by 2050, but the volume of snowfall will increase; the net effect on the ecosystem, including on hunting and herding communities, will be negative. By 2100 the area of near-surface permafrost in Canada will decline by 16–20%, with an additional 9–22% partially disappearing. Alaska is projected to see permafrost degradation in up to 57% of its territory, and Eastern Siberia is particularly susceptible to such changes. These types of changes can lead to landslides and coastal erosion, and affect populations and infrastructure. Changes in river and lake ice will reduce the severity of ice-jam flooding but increase mid-winter breakups and associated flooding. Glaciers, ice caps and the Greenland Ice Sheet will continue to melt and break up, leading to altered drainage patterns, exposure of new land, increased run-off (at least until the glaciers decline significantly) and catastrophic flooding. Contaminants and natural sediments released from the ice will affect water quality and enter the food chain. The sea-ice decline will lead to increased productivity in marine ecosystems as a whole, but will affect many species negatively. There may be increased biological productivity and biodiversity with, for example, greater phytoplankton growth in ice-free waters and increased nutrient run-off from land, and the resulting introduction of non- or sub-Arctic invertebrate, fish and bird species into new areas. However, many species are highly adapted to conditions under or on the edge of the sea ice, especially zooplankton and small fish which provide the basis of the food chain for a wide range of iconic and commercially valuable species, such as ringed seals, narwhals, polar bears, ivory gulls, Arctic cod, Atlantic cod and capelin. Some of these species may also be threatened as new disease organisms and parasites expand their ranges, or require sea ice for breeding. The precise consequences of such major disruption of ecosystems are unpredictable, but could include the drastic decline, or even extinction, of some important species.

Moreover, the decline of snow cover, river and lake ice, and permafrost, as well as sea ice in coastal areas, will make transportation to and between Arctic settlements and hunting, fishing and herding grounds more difficult and expensive. Infrastructure may need more frequent maintenance, or to be replaced entirely, and the dynamic nature and rapid rate of change will compound this problem and make planning difficult. At the same time, however, new opportunities for resource exploitation and maritime transport will also emerge (see Chapter Two).[34]

The Arctic today

At the beginning of the twenty-first century, about 4m people lived in the Arctic, approximately 10% of whom were members of indigenous groups.[35] Russians accounted for nearly half of the total Arctic population.[36] About one-third of the inhabitants of the region live in settlements with fewer than 5,000 people, while about 10% live in the five largest cities: Murmansk, Arkhangelsk, Anchorage, Norilsk and Reykjavik.[37] (Only Murmansk and Norilsk lie above the Arctic Circle; nearly half the approximately 2m people who live above the circle are in the ten largest cities, eight of which are in Russia and two of which are in Norway.)

The population of Arctic Russia more than quadrupled in the 15 years before the Second World War; much of this growth involved involuntary migration, including large numbers of prisoners. The population of all parts of the Arctic grew in the immediate post-war period, especially in Alaska, Greenland and Russia, and continued to rise until the end of the Cold War. The population of Arctic Sweden and Finland began to decline in the 1960s, and in the 1980s for Norway. Canada's Arctic population growth slowed significantly in the 1970s.[38]

The last decade of the twentieth century saw a net drop in the population of the Arctic due to migration.[39] This was most dramatic in Russia, which lost nearly a quarter of its Arctic population.[40] Between 2000 and 2005, this pan-Arctic trend continued, as the total population declined by 0.8%.[41] But these numbers mask significant differences between regions. The population of Alaska and the Canadian Arctic had continued to grow slowly during the 1990s, and grew rapidly after the turn of the century, outstripping the trend in the remainder of both countries. The population of Arctic Russia continued to decline, but more slowly than in the rest of the country, and the regions with large oil and gas industries grew at rates comparable to those in Arctic North America. Sweden and Norway saw modest drops; they were the only countries where the percentage of the overall population living in the Arctic fell.[42] These trends continued to the end of the decade, with little net change in the overall population of the Arctic between 2000 and 2010.[43] The main factor driving both the overall and sub-regional trends was economic migration.

In 2001 the total GDP equivalent of the Arctic was US$230 billion, of which two-thirds, or US$154bn, was from the Russian Arctic. The Arctic economy as a whole grew by over 31% in real terms between 2000 and 2009, while the rate of growth for the eight Arctic nations as a whole was 2.1%.[44] Again, there were significant national and regional differences. The average annual growth rate in the Arctic in 2000–05 was just over 6%, but for Russia it was nearly 8%, while for the US and Denmark it was about 1.5% and 1% respectively. In Denmark, Norway and the US, nationwide economic-growth rates were higher than those of their Arctic regions, but all other countries saw faster Arctic growth. Some parts of the Russian Arctic saw negative growth, but in the hydrocarbon-rich regions annual growth ran at 10–15%.[45] Since the economy of the Arctic relies heavily on primary-resource extraction and related service sectors, the global financial crisis and economic downturn of 2008–09 had a disproportionate impact on the region; conversely, recovery in most parts of the Arctic has been faster than in the Arctic states as a whole.

The Arctic economy is based on large-scale extractive industries, including ores; precious metals and gems; oil and gas; and fisheries and timber.[46] Primary extraction makes up about one-quarter of Arctic GDP, and over 60% of Russia's GDP. Russian activity is dominated by hydrocarbons, with significant production of gold, nickel, tin and diamonds; Alaska's production is also dominated by hydrocarbons, and it hosts the world's largest zinc mine. Canada produces a range of minerals, particularly diamonds, as well as hydrocarbons. In 2007 one-tenth of the world's oil and one-quarter of the world's gas were produced in the Arctic, with 80% and 99% respectively coming from Russia. Other important strategic minerals are also mined, although they comprise a small proportion of overall production. Greenland and the Faroe Islands are heavily reliant on fisheries. Arctic Sweden has important mineral production and Finland has forestries, but in both nations the Arctic economy also involves significant secondary industries. Extractive industries make up the smallest proportion of Arctic economic activity in Iceland, Norway and Finland. In sub-national regions with no important extractive industries, the economy tends to be subsistence-based and a significant proportion of economic activity comes from public services, which generally dominate the service sector in the Arctic. Among other service activities, transport is significant because of the distances and logistics involved in travel through the Arctic, and tourism represents a small but growing sector. Although comprising only a small proportion of the Arctic economy, activities such as meteorological services and support and control for civilian satellites in polar orbits have considerable strategic importance.

In 2004, the 'snapshot year' selected by the Arctic Marine Shipping Assessment (AMSA), at least 3,000 vessels operated in the Arctic, excluding ships following the great-circle route between North America and Asia through the Aleutian Islands. Just under half were fishing vessels, and about 20% were bulk carriers. Many of these ships would have made more than one voyage in Arctic waters during the year. The most significant activities, other than fishing, were bulk cargo, community resupply and tourism. The highest concentrations of shipping were in the Barents Sea and along the Norwegian coast (bulk cargo, oil and liquefied natural gas (LNG) carriers, coastal ferries, fishing vessels, cruise ships and smaller vessels); around Iceland and near the Faroe Islands and southwest Greenland (fishing, domestic-cargo supply and cruise ships); and in the Bering Sea (fishing, coastal-community supply and bulk cargo serving the Red Dog zinc mine). There was also significant traffic into the Kara Sea to service the Norilsk nickel mine. Most of the traffic was in waters that were either permanently or seasonally ice-free. There were no commercial voyages through the NWP, the NSR or in the Arctic Ocean proper.[47] Internal shipping on the NSR amounted to some 1.2m tonnes of goods.[48]

The number of commercial voyages and volume of cargo transiting the NSR, although still very small, has since increased dramatically. In 2010 five ships made the voyage. In 2011 the number was 41, including the first supertanker to transit the route. In 2012 there were 46 ships, including the first LNG carrier, which sailed from Hammerfest to the Japanese port of Tobata. Total commercial tonnage transiting the route in 2012 reached 1.26m tonnes, 50% higher than in 2011 and more than the internal traffic in 2004. For the first time, non-Russian-flagged vessels outnumbered Russian ships.[49] Although the route has been ice-free for at least part of the summer every year since 2008, most commercial vessels have been accompanied by an icebreaker escort.

Legal framework

This human activity in the Arctic does not occur in a legal vacuum, nor is the region sui generis from a legal perspective. The widespread perception that the Arctic is an ungoverned space stems from several factors. Along with Antarctica, it was one of the last parts of the world to be explored by European nations, whose historical relationships form the basis of customary international law. Again like Antarctica, much of the Arctic is uninhabited and uninhabitable without modern technology, and the indigenous peoples of the region were not organised into states during the period of European exploration and expansion. Competing land and maritime territorial claims among European powers for parts of the Arctic are as old as the Westphalian system itself.

Most of these disputes have been resolved, however, and the remainder are governed by international law in the form of UNCLOS.[50] The first formal international legal regime governing maritime territorial jurisdiction, sovereignty and claims stemmed from the first UN Law of the Sea conference in 1956, which resulted in a set of four treaties, agreed in 1958, that came into force between 1962 and 1966. These, however, left many issues ambiguous or unresolved, and were superseded by the 1982 convention, which came into force in 1994.

UNCLOS divides the world's oceans into a number of well-defined categories:

- *Internal waters*, on the landward side of a baseline defined either by the low-water line or, in the case of deeply indented coastlines or those with fringing islands, by straight lines between specified points.

- *Territorial seas*, extending to 12 nautical miles from the coastline (with additional provisos for archipelagic states and baseline definitions), in which coastal states may in principle enforce any law, regulate any use and exploit any resource, but must allow innocent passage of warships and merchant ships from any nation, and transit passage through international straits. Innocent passage is also permitted through internal waters defined by the straight-line method, where they had not been treated as internal before adoption of the convention.

- The *contiguous zone*, extending from 12–24nm, in which coastal states may exercise the control necessary to enforce their customs, fiscal, immigration and sanitary laws, but otherwise all states have freedom of navigation and over-flight.

- The *exclusive economic zone (EEZ)*, extending from 24–200nm, in which coastal states have sovereign rights over natural resources in the seas and seabed, including fisheries, minerals and wind and tidal power, but all states have freedom of navigation and overflight and the freedom to lay submarine cables and pipelines.

- The *high seas* beyond 200nm, in which all states have absolute freedom of operation, as long as it is for 'peaceful purposes', including freedom to fish. Mineral resources on or under the sea floor are 'the common heritage of mankind' and under the jurisdiction of the International Seabed Authority (ISA).

Of particular relevance to the Arctic, where the continental margin extends beyond 200nm, is the fact that a state may claim an extended continental shelf, covering resources on and under the sea floor only, up to 350nm, or 100nm from the point where water depth exceeds 2,500 metres – whichever is greater (Article 76). Such claims must be submitted to the Commission on the Limits of the Continental Shelf (CLCS) within ten years of acceding to the convention. States must pay a variable royalty on the value of extracted resources from the extended continental shelf to the ISA. The commission is composed of scientists and experts, makes its recommendations on the basis of scientific evidence and does not mediate between conflicting claims.

The convention encourages the diplomatic resolution of disputes, but provides for compulsory and binding arbitration through a variety of mechanisms, ranging from the International Tribunal on the Law of the Sea and the International Court of Justice to various defined and ad hoc tribunals. However, countries are allowed to opt out of such binding arbitration in a number of areas, including conflicting EEZ and continental-shelf claims. Both Russia and Canada have explicitly done so. The US has not ratified the convention but does treat its provisions with regard to navigation and territory as customary international law. In the May 2008 Ilulissat Declaration, ministers from the five Arctic littoral states noted that the 'law of the sea' provides for the delineation of the outer limits of the continental shelf, freedom of navigation and other uses of the sea, and that they remained 'committed to this legal framework and to the orderly settlement of any possible overlapping claims' and saw 'no need to develop a new comprehensive international legal regime to govern the Arctic Ocean'.[51]

Moreover, the disputes that do exist in the region are few and largely benign. There is only one unresolved land border in the Arctic, for example: the barren, 1.3km^2 Hans Island, lying almost exactly midway in the narrow (30km-wide) Nares Strait between Greenland and Ellesmere Island, is claimed by both Canada and Denmark. Ottawa asserted its claim during negotiations over the continental-shelf boundary between Canada and Greenland in 1973, and final agreement left the question of sovereignty over the island in abeyance. An 875-metre gap, stretching from the low-water line north and south of the island, was left in the more than 2,500km-long boundary. The question of who owns Hans Island has been a source of tension since 1984, with contingents of military personnel periodically being sent to reassert sovereignty in 2003 and 2004. The issue became heated in 2004, with much public posturing on both sides, before the parties agreed to reduce tension and begin negotiations towards a resolution. It is likely that the island itself has no economic value, and given that under the 1973 treaty it has no territorial sea, possession would not give either nation any more maritime territory or a larger EEZ. Its importance is purely symbolic, as an expression of national resolve with regard to other Arctic disagreements. It is thus a source of tension in direct proportion to the amount of attention it is given by the media and in public statements by officials. There were reports in 2012 that the issue might soon be resolved, possibly by a simple compromise creating a land border bisecting the island. There have also been reports that Canada is eager to resolve the dispute before its 2013 deadline for submitting a claim to ownership of an extended continental shelf in the Arctic Ocean to the CLCS, although the Hans Island dispute has no bearing on such a claim. A long-standing maritime boundary dispute between Canada and Greenland affecting about 200km² in the Lincoln Sea north of the Nares Strait was resolved in principle in November 2012.[52]

There is also, perhaps surprisingly, only a single unresolved maritime territorial dispute in the Arctic, involving the boundary between the US and Canada in the Beaufort Sea. (The US–Russia maritime border was agreed in 1990, before the collapse of the Soviet Union; it has been ratified by the US but not by Russia.) Ottawa argues that the US–Canada boundary should be an extension of the land border, which is also the direct line due north from the coast to the North Pole (although this latter factor is not a basis for Canada's claim). Washington's position is that the border should be perpendicular to the coastline, or equidistant from each nation's land territory. Since the coast runs slightly northwest–southeast at this point, and is convex, this would make the boundary run north by northeast. The disputed maritime territory, including the 200nm EEZs, amounts to some 21,000km², in an area rich in known and suspected hydrocarbon resources. The two countries are, to be sure, cooperating in a joint geological survey of the region. Moreover, through an odd quirk of geometry and the way that extended continental-shelf claims are calculated, beyond the 200nm EEZ the US interpretation of the border actually favours Canada, and vice versa. However, there are domestic political pressures in both countries that will make formal resolution of the dispute difficult.

Besides these formal territorial disputes, there are potential overlaps in extended continental-shelf claims. These are often referred to as current disputes, but so far only Norway and Russia have made formal submissions to the CLCS, and Russia's 2001 submission was returned with a request for additional research and data. Russia's expansive claim would extend the US–Russia maritime border to the North Pole, and follow the 2,500-metre depth contour towards the Siberian coast, up to the 200nm EEZ.[53] The validity of the full claim under UNCLOS depends on whether the Mendeleev and Lomonosov ridges are determined to be extensions of Russia's continental shelf – the issue on which the CLCS sought further evidence. Only in a relatively small area near the pole does Moscow's claim extend beyond the median line between Russia and Canada or Greenland. It is by no means certain that Russia's claim will eventually be validated by the CLCS, or that Ottawa or Copenhagen will submit claims up to the median line, or which overlap Russia's claim. On the other hand, it is also possible that Ottawa and Copenhagen may claim territory beyond the median line. If there is overlap between the claims, the CLCS could validate one or the other, or both. In any case, resolution of the claims can only really come through negotiation between the countries involved, unless they agree to submit them to arbitration.

Norway's 2006 claim covered three areas – the so-called 'Banana Hole' in the Norwegian Sea, the 'Loop Hole' in the Barents Sea, and the western Nansen Basin in the Arctic Ocean; Oslo reserved the right to make further submissions.[54] None of these areas overlap with potential claims from other states; parts of the Banana Hole, where Danish (Faroese), Icelandic and Norwegian claims might overlap, were the subject of a 2006 agreement pending the CLCS recommendations as to whether the area was continental shelf. In 2009 the commission confirmed that the areas in Norway's submission were in fact continental shelf.[55] The shelf boundary in the Loop Hole, an area of high seas that lies between the Russian and Norwegian EEZs and the 200nm Svalbard Fisheries Protection Zone, was the subject of a dispute between Oslo and Moscow until 2010, when it was resolved as part of a broader maritime and continental-shelf demarcation agreement, which was ratified in 2011.[56]

Three other areas of dispute stem from varying interpretations of UNCLOS and other international treaties. Two relate to maritime routes through the Arctic: Canada claims the NWP as internal waters, as does Russia for the NSR, while the US and the EU maintain that both, or parts of both, constitute international straits. There have been suggestions from Chinese academics that Beijing could take a similar position, although China's interpretation of freedom of navigation under UNCLOS in other parts of the world tends to be at odds with the transatlantic view.[57] Finally, there are conflicting interpretations of the 1920 Svalbard Treaty. Under the treaty, Norway has sovereignty over the archipelago, but citizens of other signatory nations are allowed equal (but not unrestricted) access to fisheries and mineral resources on the islands and in territorial waters. Oslo's position is that the treaty provisions are restricted to these areas, and do not apply between 12nm and 200nm off shore, which it considers part of Norway's EEZ under UNCLOS. Russia argues that Norway has no rights beyond the territorial sea, while other signatories acknowledge that Svalbard has an EEZ and continental shelf but that the provisions of the treaty apply in those zones.[58]

Non-governance: the Arctic Council

While UNCLOS provides the overarching legal framework for most transnational Arctic issues, in practice there is no organised regional governance structure. The only body that might be considered in this light, the Arctic Council, is an intergovernmental forum – a high-level talking shop – rather than an intergovernmental organisation. Other governance structures that cover the Arctic are, like UNCLOS, global (the International Maritime Organization; various trans-boundary environmental treaties) or sub-regional (bilateral agreements; regional fisheries regimes; other trans-boundary environmental treaties). Many of the sub-regional structures cover not only part of the Arctic, but substantial areas outside the Arctic as well.[59]

The Arctic Council was established in 1996 by the eight Arctic states as a 'high-level forum' to promote 'cooperation, coordination and interaction ... on common Arctic issues'.[60] It developed out of the Arctic Environmental Protection Strategy (AEPS), a non-binding 1991 agreement, and subsumed various AEPS initiatives, such as the Arctic Monitoring and Assessment Programme, Conservation of Arctic Flora and Fauna, Protection of the Arctic Marine Environment, and Emergency, Prevention, Preparedness and Response. These form four of the six working groups in which most of the council's activity occurs; the other two are the Arctic Contaminants Action Programme and the Sustainable Development Working Group. (Many of the synthesis reports and assessments cited earlier in this chapter are the products of these working groups.) Besides the eight Arctic states, six indigenous peoples' organisations are permanent non-voting participants of the council, which operates by consensus. Provision was made for observers, of whom there are now 32, including nine intergovernmental or inter-parliamentary organisations and 11 non-governmental organisations. Twelve countries – France, Germany, the Netherlands, Poland, Spain, the UK, Italy, Japan, China, South Korea, Singapore and India – have been granted observer status, the last six only in May 2013. The EU's application was deferred over Canadian objections to European policy on seal products, but this is expected to be resolved soon. Each member holds the council chair for two years, with the handover occurring at the biennial ministerial meetings, the most recent of which was held in Kiruna in May 2013. Canada was the first to hold the chair, and took over from Sweden again in 2013, to begin a second cycle. Observers engage principally through the working groups, but sit on the periphery at the ministerials.

The Arctic Council's remit remains strictly environmental and economic – a footnote in the 1996 Ottawa Declaration explicitly excludes military-security matters from the 'common Arctic issues' it covers – and it has no decision-making power. Two important treaties have been negotiated under its auspices – a search-and-rescue agreement in 2011 and an oil-spill preparedness agreement in 2013 – but they are not enforced or administered by the council or its secretariat. In fact, until May 2013, the council did not even have a permanent secretariat, and the new organisation has only five staff and a strictly limited remit.

As military-security issues remain outside the remit of the Arctic Council, some lower-level international forums have been established to cover such topics. The chiefs-of-defence staff of the eight Arctic nations met in Canada in 2012 and Greenland in 2013, and the North Pacific Coast Guard Forum, established in 2000, and North Atlantic Coast Guard Forum (NACGF), established in 2007, include parts of the broader Arctic under their remits. All eight Arctic states are members of the NACGF, but the forum's real focus is much broader. Finally, the Arctic Security Forces Roundtable is an informal gathering of senior military officers from the eight Arctic nations, plus France, Germany, the

Netherlands and the UK, which has met each year since 2011 to discuss shared challenges and exchange information and best practices on issues such as infrastructure, communications, the environment, joint exercises and training, and maritime domain awareness.

Conclusion

The Arctic has seen significant economic activity since the end of the nineteenth century, and played an important military-strategic role in the global wars of the twentieth century. In the second half of the twentieth century, there was rapid growth in economic activity and population size. Over the same time period, the Arctic climate was warming, at a rate significantly faster than that of the rest of the globe. From the middle of the twentieth century, summer sea-ice extent fell by nearly 8% per decade, with comparable declines in ice volume and thickness. Yet economic and demographic developments have been driven more by political than environmental considerations, and the High North remains sparsely populated, rarely visited and barely governed.

Rapid climatic change, both current and projected, has led to concern that the Arctic may soon become a sphere of competition and confrontation, as the political and military vacuum sucks in interested parties and actors jostle for position in what is the last of Earth's great unstructured regions. The Arctic Ocean is expected to become seasonally ice-free well before mid-century, allowing greater access to resources and requiring increasing capabilities to police and protect the region. Territorial disputes that have long remained dormant because they were of little political relevance are now being seen as potential sources of tension. But whether the Arctic will become a region of competition, as states jockey for favourable positions and seek to maximise territorial claims, will largely depend on the economic viability of the High North, and the geographical distribution of economic opportunities within the region. The next chapter discusses the potential for discovery and development of new mineral resources, especially oil and gas; changes in agriculture, forestry and fisheries; and the exploitation of newly accessible maritime routes in the Arctic for commerce and tourism in the context of regional climate change and global economic trends.

Notes

1 See Oran R. Young and Niels Einarsson, 'Introduction: Human Development in the Arctic', in *Arctic Human Development Report* (Akureyri: Stefansson Arctic Institute, 2004), pp. 22–6.

2 Broadly speaking, there are two main related indigenous groups (or language families) in the High North: Inuit (Greenland, Canada and Alaska) and Yupik (Alaska and Eastern Siberia). The term 'Eskimo' is often used in Alaska, and by linguists and anthropologists, as an umbrella term to encompass both groups. Many Inuit in Canada and Greenland, however, view 'Eskimo' as offensive, and 'Inuit' is often also used to refer to all circumpolar indigenous groups, for example in the charter of the Inuit Circumpolar Council.

3 For greater detail on the prehistory of the Arctic, see John F. Hoffecker, *A Prehistory of the North: human settlement of the higher latitudes* (New Brunswick, NJ, and London: Rutgers University Press, 2005); Richard Vaughan, *The Arctic: A History* (Stroud: Alan Sutton, 2007).

4 Frederic G. Cassidy and Richard N. Ringler (eds), *Bright's Old English Grammar and Reader*, (New York: Holt, Rinehart and Winston, 1971), pp. 184–91; Irmeli Valtonen, 'An Interpretation of the Description of Northernmost Europe in the Old English *Orosius*', University of Oulu, August 1988, http://www.helsinki.fi/varieng/people/valtonen/MAthesis.pdf.

5 Sophia Perdikaris and Thomas H. McGovern, 'Viking Age Economics and the Origins of Commercial Cod Fisheries in the North Atlantic', in Louis Sickling and Darlene Abreu-Ferreira (eds), *Beyond the Catch: Fisheries of the North Atlantic, the North Sea and the Baltic, 900–1950* (Leiden: Brill, 2008), pp. 61–90.

6 The terms 'Northeast Passage' (NEP) and 'Northwest Passage' reflect a European perspective and derive from the Age of Exploration in the 15th–17th centuries. The term 'Northern Sea Route' (NSR) is often used today, especially by Russians, instead of 'Northeast Passage'. Strictly speaking, however, the NSR is an administrative entity comprising the seaways under Russian jurisdiction between Novaya Zemlya and the Bering Strait, excluding the Barents, Pechora and White seas. It was defined in Soviet legislation in 1932 and 1976, and in subsequent Russian laws, taking into account the definitions of national waters

and EEZs under the 1982 UN Convention on the Law of the Sea. This book uses NEP in historical contexts, or when referring to the entire route between the Atlantic and the Bering Strait.

7 For a comprehensive survey of these efforts, see Fergus Fleming, *Barrow's Boys* (London: Granta, 1998); and Vaughan, *The Arctic: A History*, pp. 144–69. For other countries' Arctic efforts in this period, see *Ibid.*, pp. 170–200; and Fergus Fleming, *Ninety Degrees North* (London: Granta, 2001).

8 Grégoire Côte and Michelle Picard-Aitken, *Arctic Research in Canada: A bibliometric analysis* (Montreal: Science-Metric, 2009), pp. 6–7.

9 See Francis Spufford, *I May Be Some Time* (London: Faber and Faber, 1996); Young and Einarsson, 'Introduction: Human Development in the Arctic', pp. 23–6.

10 Vaughan, *The Arctic: A History*, pp. 201–2.

11 'NSR Transits before 2011', ARCTIS Knowledge Hub, Centre for High North Logistics, http://www.arctis-search.com/NSR+Transits+before+2011&structure=Arctic+Sea+Routes.

12 AMAP, 'Arctic Climate Issues 2011: Changes in Arctic Snow, Water, Ice and Permafrost', SWIPA 2011 Overview Report, 20 December 2012, p. 30.

13 *Ibid.*, p. 24.

14 Leonid Polyak et al., 'History of sea ice in the Arctic', *Quaternary Science Reviews*, vol. 29, no. 15–16, July 2010, pp. 1,757–78.

15 National Snow and Ice Data Center, 'Sea Ice Index', http://nsidc.org/data/seaice_index/.

16 Gifford H. Miller et al., 'Temperature and precipitation history of the Arctic', *Quaternary Science Reviews*, vol. 29, no. 15–16, July 2010, pp. 1679–715.

17 Polyak et al., 'History of sea ice in the Arctic'.

18 Miller et al., 'Temperature and precipitation history of the Arctic'. For a more detailed discussion of the cooling trend over the last two millennia, see Darrell S. Kaufman et al., 'Recent Warming Reverses Long-Term Arctic Cooling', *Science*, vol. 325, no. 5,945, September 2009, pp. 1,236–9.

19 IPCC, 'Climate Change 2013: The Physical Science Basis', Working Group I Contribution to the Fifth Assessment Report, Technical Summary, June 2013, p. TS-5, http://www.ipcc.ch/report/ar5/wg1/. (Approved draft to be read in conjunction with IPCC, 'Climate Change 2013: The Physical Science Basis – Changes to the Underlying Scientific/Technical Assessment', Working Group I Contribution to the Fifth Assessment Report, 26 September 2013.)

20 *Ibid.*

21 IPCC, 'Climate Change 2007: Impacts, Adaptation and Vulnerability', Working Group II Contribution to the Fourth Assessment Report, pp. 656–7.

22 Julienne Stroeve et al., 'Arctic sea ice decline: Faster than forecast', *Geophysical Research Letters*, vol. 34, no. 9, 1 May 2007; Stroeve et al., 'Trends in Arctic sea ice extent from CMIP5, CMIP3 and observations', *Geophysical Research Letters*, vol. 39, no. 16, 28 August 2012.

23 AMAP, 'Arctic Climate Issues 2011'.

24 Kaufman et al., 'Recent Warming Reverses Long-Term Arctic Cooling'; National Snow and Ice

Data Center, 'Sea Ice Index', http://nsidc.org/data/g02135.html. The summer minimum ice extent and volume in 2012 were the lowest on record. The lowest winter maximum extent on record came in 2011, but the ten lowest maxima have all been in the last ten years, and the three lowest winter maximum ice-volume years were 2012, 2013 and 2011. For the most up-to-date survey of environmental conditions and changes in the Arctic, see Martin O. Jeffries et al. (eds), 'Arctic Report Card 2012', National Oceanic and Atmospheric Administration, 2012.

25 IPCC, 'Climate Change 2007: The Physical Science Basis', Working Group I Contribution to the Fourth Assessment Report, pp. 904–5.

26 Xiangdong Zhang and John E. Walsh, 'Toward a Seasonally Ice-Covered Arctic Ocean: Scenarios from the IPCC AR4 Model Simulations', *Journal of Climate*, vol. 19, no. 9, 1 May 2006, pp. 1,730–47.

27 'Arctic sea ice extent settles at record seasonal minimum', National Snow and Ice Data Center, 19 September 2012, http://nsidc.org/arcticseaicenews/2012/09/arctic-sea-ice-extent-settles-at-record-seasonal-minimum/.

28 Stroeve et al., 'Arctic sea ice decline: Faster than forecast'. See also IPCC, 'Climate Change 2013', Technical Summary, pp. TS-51–TS-52.

29 Muyin Wang and James E. Overland, 'A sea ice free summer Arctic within 30 years?', *Geophysical Research Letters*, vol. 36, no. 7, 3 April 2009.

30 Wang and Overland, 'A sea ice free summer Arctic within 30 years – An update from CMIP5 models', *Geophysical Research Letters*, vol. 39, no. 18, 25 September 2012.

31 Overland and Wang, 'When will the summer Arctic be nearly ice free?', *Geophysical Research Letters*, vol. 40, no. 10, 21 May 2013.

32 'Diplomatic shifts in the warming Arctic', IISS *Strategic Comments*, vol. 16, no. 50, December 2010.

33 For an up-to-date summary of the scientific understanding of Arctic sea-ice trends, see Stroeve et al., 'The Arctic's rapidly shrinking sea ice cover: a research synthesis', *Climatic Change*, vol. 110, no. 3–4, February 2012, pp. 1,005–27.

34 This paragraph summary is based on ch. 12, 'SWIPA synthesis: implications of findings', in AMAP, 'Snow, Water, Ice and Permafrost in the Arctic (SWIPA): Climate Change and the Cryosphere', SWIPA Scientific Assessment Report, 2011.

35 Dmitry Bogoyavlenskiy and Andy Siggner, 'Arctic Demography', in *Arctic Human Development Report* (Akureyri: Stefansson Arctic Institute, 2004), p. 27.

36 *Ibid.*, pp. 27–42.

37 AMAP, 'Snow, Water, Ice and Permafrost in the Arctic (SWIPA)', ch. 10, pp. 1,310–14.

38 Bogoyavlenskiy and Siggner, 'Arctic Demography', p. 29.

39 *Ibid.*, p. 27.

40 *Ibid.*, p. 29.

41 Solveig Glomsrød and Iulie Aslaksen (eds), 'The Economy of the North 2008', *Statistics Analyses*, Statistics Norway, November 2009, pp. 28–9. Glomsrød and Aslaksen use a much broader definition of Arctic territory in Russia; their figure for the total population of the Arctic is consequently more than twice that of the AHDR, and the proportion of the total Arctic population living in Russia is

accordingly closer to 75% than 50%.

42 *Ibid.*

43 Sustainable Development Working Group, 'Arctic Human Development Report II: Regional Processes & Global Linkages Fact Sheet', January 2013, http://www.arctic-council.org/index.php/en/document-archive/category/446-sdwg.

44 *Ibid.*

45 Glomsrød and Aslaksen (eds), *'The Economy of the North 2008'*, pp. 30–1.

46 This discussion of the Arctic economy is based on AMAP, 'Snow, Water, Ice and Permafrost in the Arctic (SWIPA)', pp. 10–16; Gérard Duhaime et al., 'Economic systems', in *Arctic Human Development Report*, November 2004, pp. 69–84; Glomsrød and Aslaksen (eds), 'The Economy of the North 2008', p. 66.

47 Arctic Council, 'Arctic Marine Shipping Assessment 2009 Report', pp. 72–91.

48 'NSR Transits before 2011', Centre for High North Logistics (CHNL), http://www.arctis-search.com/NSR+Transits+before+2011&structure=Arctic+Sea+Routes.

49 'NSR Transits before 2011', 'NSR Transits 2011' and 'NSR Transits 2012', CHNL, http://www.arctis-search.com/Statistics+on+NSR+Transit+Voyages&structure=Arctic+Sea+Routes. The figures for number of ships include those repositioning or in ballast. The numbers as reported by the CHNL derive from various sources and may not be entirely accurate or directly comparable year on year. For 2012 the Norwegian Joint Headquarters, which monitors maritime traffic in the Arctic, said there were 53

rather than 46 transits (personal communication); see Jeffrey Mazo, 'Northern exposure', Politics and Strategy: The Survival Editors' Blog, 11 June 2013, http://www.iiss.org/en/politics%20and%20strategy/blogsections/2013-98d0/june-dc8b/northern-exposure-77cd.

50 UNCLOS is sometimes used to refer to the three UN *conferences* on the law of the sea between 1958 and 1982, rather than the resulting *convention*. This can cause some slight confusion. We use the acronym only in the latter sense here.

51 'The Ilulissat Declaration', Arctic Ocean Conference, Ilulissat, Greenland, 28 May 2008, http://www.oceanlaw.org/downloads/arctic/Ilulissat_Declaration.pdf.

52 Canadian Department of Foreign Affairs, Trade and Development, 'Canada and Kingdom of Denmark Reach Tentative Agreement on Lincoln Sea Boundary', news release, 28 November 2012.

53 CLCS, 'Submission by the Russian Federation', 20 December 2001, http://www.un.org/Depts/los/clcs_new/submissions_files/submission_rus.htm; Arctic Council, 'The Ottawa Declaration of 1996', 19 September 1996, http://www.arctic-council.org/index.php/en/document-archive/category/4-founding-documents.

54 CLCS, 'Submission by the Kingdom of Norway', 27 November 2006, http://www.un.org/depts/los/clcs_new/submissions_files/submission_nor.htm.

55 CLCS, 'Summary of the Recommendations of the CLCS, in Regard to the Submission made by Norway in Respect of the Areas

in the Arctic Ocean, the Barents Sea and the Norwegian Sea on 27 November 2006', 27 March 2009, http://www.un.org/depts/los/clcs_new/submissions_files/nor06/nor_rec_summ.pdf.

56 'Treaty between the Kingdom of Norway and the Russian Federation concerning Maritime Delimitation and Cooperation in the Barents Sea and the Arctic Ocean', 15 September 2010, http://www.regjeringen.no/upload/ud/vedlegg/folkerett/avtale_engelsk.pdf.

57 David Curtis Wright, 'The Dragon Eyes the Top of the World: Arctic Policy Debate and Discussion in China', China Maritime Study no. 8, US Naval War College, August 2011; Margaret Blunden, 'Geopolitics and the Northern Sea Route', International Affairs, vol. 88, no. 1, January 2012, pp. 115–29.

58 Lotta Numminen, 'A history and functioning of the Spitsbergen Treaty', in Diana Wallis and Stewart Arnold (eds), The Spitsbergen Treaty: Multilateral Governance in the Arctic, Arctic Papers, vol. 1, 2011, pp. 11–15.

59 Olav Schram Stokke, 'Political stability and Multi-level Governance in the Arctic', in Paul Arthur Berkman and Alexander N. Vylegzhanin (eds), Environmental Security in the Arctic Ocean (Dordrecht: Springer, 2010), pp. 297–312.

60 Arctic Council, 'The Ottawa Declaration of 1996'.

CHAPTER TWO

Economic opportunities

The Arctic is often described as a vast storehouse of resources –
oil and natural gas, other minerals, fisheries and forests - worth
trillions of dollars. The prospect that climate change will permit
increased exploration for, and exploitation of, these presumed
resources has generated a great deal of interest among governments, businesses, the public and the media. The seasonal decline
of sea-ice cover has also raised the prospect of large-scale maritime trade via Arctic routes that would provide great savings in
distance and time, and hence cost. Yet despite the long history of
resource extraction and navigation in the High North outlined in
the previous chapter, many known mineral deposits and other
resources are not being exploited, and trans-Arctic maritime
trade is still relatively insignificant. Barriers to further exploration, exploitation and expansion are not just physical. They are
also economic, political (in terms of both national policies and
international relations) and cultural. Some resources are known
or suspected but not competitive to extract, due to the high cost
of operations in the Arctic; some areas are, or were until recently,
disputed between Arctic nations, while still others are undisputed but have not been released for exploration by national
authorities due to environmental or other concerns. Finally,

local indigenous populations have concerns over both ownership of resources and effects on traditional ways of life. Most
of the non-indigenous population of the Arctic is there, directly
or indirectly, because of resource industries, and most of the
secondary economic benefits of those industries accrue outside
the region. This chapter explores the potential for, timing of, and
possible roadblocks to, new opportunities for resource extraction, tourism and maritime shipping routes.

Energy

The greatest part of current economic activity and investment in the Arctic involves oil and natural-gas extraction,
and hydrocarbons make up the bulk, by value, of potentially exploitable resources. Currently, about 10% of global
oil production and 25% of gas production takes place in the
Arctic; 97% of this oil and gas production comes from onshore
fields in Russia and Alaska. In 2004, about 80% of the oil and
99% of the gas produced in the Arctic was in Russia. Smaller
amounts are produced in Canada and Norway, including
the latter's offshore Snøhvit gas field, which came on-stream
in 2007.[1] By 2007, more than 400 oil and gas fields had been
discovered north of the Arctic Circle, of which 60 were extensive (containing more than 500 million boe). The discovered
fields contain 40 billion barrels of oil, 1.14 trillion cubic feet of
natural gas and 8bn barrels of natural-gas liquids – holding the
energy equivalent of 240bn barrels of oil and comprising 10%
of global cumulative hydrocarbon production and remaining
proved reserves.[2] One-quarter of the known fields are not yet
in production, most of them in North America.[3]

The number of exploratory wells drilled in the Arctic peaked
in the late 1980s with the development of Russia's onshore
resources and began to increase again near the beginning of the
twenty-first century. The total area open to exploration has also
steadily increased, but because the Soviet Union lacked a system

for the conveyance of commercial rights, the trend is difficult to establish.[4] Overall production of oil and gas in the Arctic has remained relatively stable since the late 1980s.[5]

In 2008 the United States Geological Survey (USGS) estimated that undiscovered conventional oil and gas north of the Arctic Circle amounted to about 90bn barrels of oil, 1.67tr cubic feet of natural gas and 44bn barrels of natural-gas liquids, equivalent to 412bn barrels of oil. (These estimates exclude non-conventional resources, such as oil shales, tar sands and gas hydrates.) Some 84% of the undiscovered resources are expected to be found offshore under less than 500 metres of water, with 70% of the undiscovered oil in five geological provinces in or off Alaska, Canada, Greenland and Russia (specifically, the East Barents Sea) and an equivalent proportion of gas in or off Russia and Alaska (primarily, Russia). The south Kara Sea alone is estimated to contain almost 39% of the undiscovered gas. The total estimated resources amount to about 30% of the world's undiscovered gas and 13% of its undiscovered oil, or 4% of the world's remaining, conventionally recoverable oil resources.[6] These estimates are of hydrocarbons recoverable using existing technology, without reference to ocean depth or ice cover; they also exclude any economic considerations, including global price levels and costs of exploration and development. A commercial energy research and analysis company estimates that offshore hydrocarbon reserves – as opposed to resources – in the wider Arctic amount to 17bn barrels of oil and 116bn boe of natural gas, 82% of which is in Russia.[7]

Estimates by the USGS have formed the basis of almost all the reporting and discussion of Arctic energy potential over the last few years. They are, however, nothing more than educated, if highly rigorous, guesses. They are based on a probabilistic, model-based comparison of Arctic sub-regions with other parts of the world with similar geologies and known oil resources. Thus, there is a high degree of uncertainty in the reported figures, which are averages of 50,000 model runs. For example, the mean figure for undiscovered oil was 90bn barrels, but while there is a greater than 95% probability that there are more than 44bn barrels, there is only a 50% chance that there are more than 83bn barrels and a 5% chance that there are more than 157bn barrels. The story is the same for natural gas: a mean of nearly 1,669tr cubic feet masks a 50% chance that there is more than 1,500tr cubic feet, with the 5–95% range running from 770–2,990tr cubic feet.[8]

Since the USGS estimates only cover regions north of the Arctic Circle, the situation for the larger Arctic, as defined by AMAP or the AHDR, is more difficult to assess. Prior to the release of the USGS 2008 estimates, remaining discovered, proven or probable oil reserves in the broader US, Canadian, Norwegian and Russian Arctic (therefore excluding Greenland) amounted to over 130bn barrels, and remaining gas to 1,530tr cubic feet, for a total of 390bn boe.[9] This is less than the mean of 412bn boe from the 2008 USGS assessment for north of the Arctic Circle alone, which represents a significant increase in estimated resources. The geological provinces containing the bulk of the putative undiscovered offshore resources are, to be sure, all north of the circle, with the exception of the Labrador Sea, which covers part of the West Greenland–East Canada Province. The most recent estimate for this province suggests a mean of 10.7bn barrels of oil, 75tr cubic feet of gas and 1.7bn barrels of natural-gas liquids, of which 7.3bn, 52tr and 1.1bn lie north of the Arctic Circle.[10] The offshore resources in the wider Arctic amount to only 1–2% of the estimated reserves in the USGS assessment. Similarly, the West Siberian Basin contains nearly one-third of the estimated undiscovered hydrocarbon resources north of the Arctic Circle, including the natural-gas resources in the Kara Sea. Inclusion of the parts of the basin that lie south of the circle, but within the AMAP or the AHDR Arctics, adds no more than 10% to the estimated oil resources and 1–2% to the gas.[11]

Exploration licences have been granted in the Beaufort, Chukchi and Labrador seas, and Baffin Bay, but drilling attempts off Alaska and Greenland in the last few years have been limited, unsuccessful, or fruitless. In May 2013, the new government of Greenland imposed a moratorium on granting further licences in its waters, including parts of the Greenland Sea for which applications had been due by October. In June, Norway awarded additional licences for exploration in parts of the Barents Sea, and plans to award licences in the sectors formally disputed with Russia in 2015. Norway's Snøhvit gas field in the Barents Sea came on-stream in 2007, and the first Barents oil field, Goliat, is due to begin production in 2014, after some delays. Two new oil fields, Skrugard and Havis (now collectively called the Johan Castberg field), were discovered in 2011–12, with an estimated 400m–600m barrels of recoverable oil. Commercial operations could begin as early as 2018. Russian companies, in conjunction with various partners, are pursuing projects in the Barents and Pechora seas, and have exploration licenses covering 125,000km^2 in parts of the Kara Sea currently covered by sea ice for 270–300 days of the year. Exploratory activity has identified formations holding 18.7bn boe in the ice-free southern Barents Sea and 7bn boe further north. Additional seismic exploration is due up until 2018 and the first exploratory wells are scheduled for 2021 and 2026.[12]

Current exploratory activity is confined to the five geological provinces expected to contain the bulk of the undiscovered hydro-carbon resources in the Arctic, and development and production are still restricted to areas such as the Barents Sea with at least 30 years' history of petroleum activity. The slow pace of current development is due to the difficulties and comparatively high cost of operating in the Arctic environment, especially offshore. It can cost between two and ten times as much to develop an oil or gas field in the Arctic than in more benign parts of the world.[13] Arctic conditions often lead to delays and cost overruns, so the timetables discussed above may be unrealistic. The average lag for Arctic oil between discovery and going on-stream is more than 13 years, the second-longest in the world.[14] Snøhvit took 17 years from discovery to development plan, and another six years to the start of production. Goliat took three years from licence to discovery, nine years from discovery to development plan, which was completed in 2009, and, although production was scheduled to begin in 2013, it has now been delayed. Russia's Shtokman gas field in the Barents Sea, the largest in the world, was discovered in 1988, but despite exploratory wells, multiple plans and shifting consortia dating back to the 1990s, development has been repeatedly postponed and a decision on whether to proceed has now been put off to at least 2014. The 530m-barrel Prirazlomnoye oil field in the Pechora Sea, which would have been the first commercial offshore field in the Arctic, was discovered in 1989, and was originally scheduled to come on-stream in 2001. It, too, has been repeatedly delayed, most recently to the last quarter of 2013, at the earliest. Given the project's recent history, there is no assurance that this date will be met either.

The difficulties of exploiting energy resources in the Arctic include the distance to markets and suppliers; lack of infrastructure; seasonal restrictions on operations, due to ice and extreme weather conditions, a lack of daylight in winter and onshore transportation difficulties due to surface thawing in summer; high cost of labour, due to the distances and conditions; uncertainty about the long-term price of oil and gas; stringent national environmental regulations, due to the fragile nature of Arctic ecosystems and in response to the 2010 Macondo disaster in the Gulf of Mexico; and energy companies' concerns that a major oil spill similar to that disaster could be a 'company-killing event'. Limited progress has had more to do with advances in technology and techniques and to energy prices than to any increased accessibility due to climate change. Recent delays in developing Shtokman, for example, are related more to the development of shale gas and lower LNG prices than to the difficulties of operating in the Arctic. The fact that many known large Arctic oil and gas fields, particularly in North America, have not been developed reflects this sensitivity to market forces and suggests that undiscovered resources may turn out to be less important than often assumed, even if they become more accessible.[15] Many of Russia's onshore fields, although profitable now, would probably not have been developed in the 1970s and 1980s if the Soviet Union had had a market-based economy.[16] The lag between beginning of exploration and beginning of production, the sensitivity to market forces and uncertainties in the long-term price of oil, and the prospect that demand for oil and gas may start to decline after 2030 or so if decarbonisation efforts to combat climate change are successful, combine to make Arctic energy less of a game changer than is often asserted or reported. Using the USGS estimates for undiscovered resources, a 2009 study concluded that at a nominal oil-price level of US$80 a barrel, Arctic oil production would never rebound to 1980s levels, but would begin to decline and would fall from 10% to 7% of world production by 2030. Natural-gas production would also decline, and fall from 21% to 9% of world production. With oil prices at US$120 a barrel, Arctic oil would continue to comprise 11–12% of world production up to 2030.[17] Despite all these barriers, the huge potential for hydrocarbon discoveries in the warming Arctic has meant sustained interest from governments, energy companies and civil-society groups that oppose further exploration and exploitation.

Even with rising temperatures and the decline of sea ice, however, it is not inevitable, or even likely, that climate change will improve access to Arctic energy resources. In fact, the reverse may be the case. University of California, Los Angeles geographer Scott Stephenson and his colleagues have used an Arctic Transport Accessibility Model to calculate that by mid-century (2045–59), most of the Arctic Ocean will become accessible to ice-strengthened ships for eight months of the year, with a 23–24% increase in accessibility of ocean area (averaged over the year) within current and claimed EEZs. The variation among the five littoral Arctic states' national territory is considerable: increases of 2% for Norway, 5% for the United States (11% for its extended claims), 16% (or 29%) for Russia, 19% (or 32%) for Canada and 28% (or 37%) for Greenland. But land transportation in the Arctic normally relies on cheap, easily constructed 'ice roads' on frozen ground, lakes and rivers, which are open for about eight months of the year. Transportation is thus much more difficult in the summer – the opposite of the maritime pattern – and conditions make summer road construction particularly complicated and expensive. In some parts of the Arctic, the period of the year in which such roads are viable has already shortened considerably, and Stephenson and colleagues calculate that milder temperatures and increased snowfall in winter will reduce the average accessible land area in the Arctic by 14% (82% for Iceland, 51% for Norway, 46% for Sweden, 41% for Finland, 29% for the US and 11–13% for Canada, Russia and Greenland).[18] These calculations exclude impacts on permanent infrastructure, such as thawing permafrost or snow accumulations on permanent roads and buildings. Other compounding factors include increased coastal erosion as sea ice declines; increased flooding from snow and ice melt; and reduced ability to use sea ice as a means of local, non-maritime travel.[19] Thus, while some offshore areas will become more accessible for exploration – to the extent that the ability to exploit particular resources depends on land-based infrastructure such as port facilities, roads, rail, pipelines and so on – the resources themselves may not be any more accessible than at present, or will require considerable investment in expensive infrastructure.

It is also important to note that the concept of a 'race for resources' in the Arctic is undermined by the location of the vast majority (90–95%) of offshore oil and gas in already demarcated

EEZs.[20] While companies and states may be eager to exploit these resources sooner rather than later, the lack of competition among states makes it unnecessary to exploit them 'first', before another actor gets there.

Non-energy resources and industries

If estimates of potential undiscovered energy resources in the Arctic are laden with uncertainty, the situation is even more pronounced for minerals such as nickel, gold, zinc, lead, palladium, platinum, rare earths and gemstones. For these non-petroleum minerals, no assessments of the scale or sophistication of the USGS Circum-Arctic Resource Appraisal (CARA) have been published. The US Arctic strategy suggests that the value of these resources amounts to more than US$1tr, but this is likely to be accurate only to within an order of magnitude.[21] Nevertheless, for many minerals, including palladium, gem- and industrial-quality diamonds, platinum, apatite, cobalt, nickel and tungsten, the Arctic provides a greater or equivalent proportion of total global production than it does for hydrocarbons (see Table 2.1). Because production volume and value are extremely sensitive to short-term price and economic fluctuations, and the most comprehensive regional figures available date from before the 2008 global financial crisis, up-to-date figures are difficult to compare on a national or sub-regional basis, and a single snapshot can be misleading in any case. Nevertheless, it appears that the biggest prospect for increased non-energy mineral production in the Arctic is through expansion of existing mines and mining regions. As is the case for oil and gas, many known reserves are not currently exploited because of market prices, inaccessibility or difficulty of operating in the region.

In 2005, mining and quarrying of non-petroleum minerals in Alaska comprised 4% of non-petroleum mineral production in the US and 4% of Alaska's Arctic gross regional product (GRP) (see Table 2.2).[22] Meanwhile, the sector comprised 20% of the Canadian Arctic GRP. As both countries' Arctic economies accounted for an insignificant proportion of national GDP, so too did their Arctic mining sectors. Only for Russia and Greenland did Arctic mining account for a noticeable percentage of GDP. In absolute terms, at US$4.2bn, the value of Russia's Arctic mining exceeds that of the rest of the region combined, and only for the US, Canada and Sweden did it exceed US$1bn. Although non-petroleum minerals make up Russia's second-largest export sector, after oil and gas, figures for the amount of this production coming from the Arctic – let alone the proportion of discovered reserves and resources – are unavailable. The richest areas are found on the Kola Peninsula, which is home to large reserves of nickel, copper, aluminium, titanium, phosphates, apatite and iron. Other parts of northwest Russia contain large reserves of bauxite and diamonds,[23] while Arctic Russia contains 10% of global palladium reserves.[24]

The issues surrounding non-petroleum minerals in the Arctic are broadly similar to those pertaining to the energy sector. Although the value varies among commodities, the reserves-to-production ratio for most minerals, including oil and gas, has remained essentially level over the last three decades.[25] The question is not so much whether vast undiscovered Arctic resources exist, but whether they will be competitive with known or undiscovered resources elsewhere on the planet. There are also significant differences between the sectors. The supply of metals in the Earth's crust is almost unrestricted compared to oil and gas, although, of course, most of this may never become economic to produce. Moreover, unlike oil and gas, many minerals, especially metals, are not consumed but can be recycled, a process that is becoming increasingly competitive with extraction. While most of the putative petroleum resources in the Arctic are located offshore, making the decline in sea ice a significant factor in accessibility for exploration, extraction and transport, offshore mining of other minerals on continental shelves is still in its infancy, and in the deep sea it is embryonic. If the technology of such mining improves to the point that it becomes economic, newly accessible offshore resources elsewhere in the world will likely make mining in the more environmentally sensitive and difficult operating conditions of the Arctic less attractive. And, as discussed above, climate change is likely, on balance, to make land-based resources in the Arctic less, not more, accessible than they are at present. Mining will also be affected by the need to invest in infrastructure for waste disposal to avoid environmental contamination as the permafrost melts.[26]

It is illuminating to examine one particular group of minerals: the rare-earth oxides. The rare-earth elements (REEs) are a group of 17 chemically related or similar elements with unique metallurgical, catalytic, electrical, magnetic and optical properties. They have hundreds of industrial uses; for many of them there are no known alternatives. They range from the high-tech – in electronic displays, information and communications technology, magnets, and batteries – to the low-tech in glass polishing. Their use has been growing significantly in the last few decades, and they are required for many new technologies that will be essential to reducing greenhouse-gas emissions and mitigating climate change globally.[27] In recent years they have also garnered a great deal of attention as critical or strategic resources for the economy and national security, for which there is a concentration of supply in a small number of mines or countries with the potential for disruption (from industrial accidents, sabotage or deliberate policy). In 2009, for example, 95% of the global REE production of 126,230 tonnes of total rare-earth oxides (TREO) came from China, with most of the rest coming from Commonwealth of Independent States (CIS) nations and India. Rare-earth elements are therefore particularly interesting in the Arctic context, not only in their own right but as a case study for the dynamics of other putative Arctic mineral resources.

Until the 1980s, the principal source of REEs was the Mountain Pass mine in California. China became the dominant supplier in 1991, and Mountain Pass shut down in 1998 for environmental reasons and because of price competition from the country. It still contains significant reserves, amounting to 13% of the world total, against China's 36% share.[28] Most REE extraction is a by-product of other mining activity; China's largest REE source, Bayan Obo in Inner Mongolia, which accounts for about half of its production, was only discovered when steel from the iron produced there was found to be contaminated with rare earths. The rest of China's output comes from a large number of smaller mines and some medium producers, mostly in the south of the country. For some of these mines, REEs are the primary product.[29] Before it shut down, however, Mountain Pass had been the only mine that produced REEs as its raison d'être. As much as 90% of global production may occur as a by-product of the extraction of other minerals.[30] Production of REE is thus less sensitive to demand than are other minerals.

China began imposing export restrictions on REEs in 2005, eventually reducing its proportion of exports by half, to about 25%, citing declining productivity, environmental problems and increasing domestic demand. Many observers suggested that Beijing could use its near-monopoly on production as a geopolitical tool, and it appears to have done so at least once, in 2010, during a period of high tension in the dispute with Japan over the Senkaku/Diaoyu islands in the East China Sea.[31] Despite China's dominance of REE production for more than a decade, major new prospecting efforts worldwide only began in 2008.

Known and inferred resources, excluding those in China, Russia and North Korea (for which no data are available), which have the potential to contribute to world supply in the short-to-medium term, amount to 14m tonnes of TREO, or 110 years' worth of supply at 2009 production rates.[32] Of this, 1.2m tonnes are at Mountain Pass, which overcame its environmental problems and reopened in January 2013, with an expected annual production of 19,000 tonnes and the capacity to expand this to 40,000 tonnes.[33] Some 3.3m tonnes are in Australia. However, 64% of REE resources are in the Arctic. Canada has 4.1m tonnes, almost all of it at Thor Lake and Strange Lake, and Greenland holds 4.9m tonnes at Kvanefjeld. All of these sites are south of the Arctic Circle, but within the Arctic as defined by the AHDR. There may, of course, be unknown deposits elsewhere in the Arctic, but they are no more likely than suspected resources in Australia, Brazil and Vietnam, which dwarf known and inferred global resources.[34] (Since these figures were collated in 2010, the owners of Kvanefjeld and Mountain Pass have upgraded their estimates by more than 100% and 36% respectively.)[35]

Rare-earth elements tend to co-occur with radioactive ores – the main source of the problems that led to the closure of Mountain Pass – and Kvanefjeld also contains large, economic amounts of uranium that are significant on a global scale. Denmark has had a zero-tolerance policy on the mining of uranium for 25 years, but Greenland obtained full authority over its natural resources in 2009 as part of its home rule. The same new government, elected in April 2013, that has put a moratorium on further licences for offshore energy exploration lifted the ban in October 2013, allowing the Kvanefjeld project to proceed. Production is expected to begin by 2017.[36]

Global supply of REEs actually outstrips demand at present, and projections suggest that this will remain the case until at least 2025, taking into account mines and refineries coming online in the next few years.[37] But not all REEs are equal; they have different uses and every deposit contains different proportions of the 17 elements. Major shortfalls of neodymium and dysprosium, critical for electric vehicle batteries and wind turbines, among other things, are projected to occur.[38] Particularly because of environmental issues, the time needed to develop and begin production at a new REE mine is comparable to that for developing a new oil or gas field.[39] Kvanefjeld is particularly rich in the less common 'heavy REEs', including dysprosium, as well as in neodymium (a light REE). Although it is comprised of relatively low-grade ores compared to existing mines, the nature of the ore may make it easier to process, and, even without the profit from uranium as a by-product, the cost of REE production will be close to that for existing Chinese producers.[40]

The situation with regard to REEs illustrates the difficulties of identifying trends and opportunities for Arctic resource exploitation. Top-line figures for the size and value of resources can be misleading, and every resource and deposit needs to be treated on an individual basis, in the context of other Arctic deposits; other reserves and resources worldwide; viability for extraction; access; demand projections; and so on.

Fisheries and forestry

Other significant Arctic resources and industries that may be affected by climate change include fisheries, forestry and tourism. The Arctic currently provides about 5% of the global fish catch.[41] But only for Greenland, Iceland and the Faroe Islands – all of which lie entirely within the Arctic under our working definition – does Arctic fishing account for a significant percentage of national GDP, and among the other Arctic nations only Russia gains more than 1% of total GDP from the sector (see Table 2.2). It is difficult to project how climate change will affect Arctic fisheries; beyond the uncertainties surrounding the rate and extent of climate change itself, climate models do not include many variables that significantly influence fish stocks. In the longer term, freshwater fisheries are likely to be adversely affected, while stocks of some commercially valuable marine species could increase and others could decline, with changes in the geographical distribution of the fisheries.[42] On balance, the impact of climate change on fisheries to the end of the twenty-first century is unlikely to have significant, long-term socio-economic effects on a national level; fisheries-management policy and practices, and their enforcement, will be more important.[43] It is on the level of local communities that impacts on oceanic fish stocks and freshwater fisheries will be most strongly felt.[44] This may be balanced by better conditions for subsistence agriculture, but availability of water will be a constraint.[45] This dynamic will also be reflected in Arctic forestry, but in this case it is even more difficult to project the impact of climate change than it is for fish.[46] Yet only in Finland and Sweden – the two mainland non-littoral Arctic states – do forestry, wood and paper manufacturing make up more than 2% of their Arctic economies, and only for Finland does the sector make a noticeable contribution to national GDP (Table 2.2).

Tourism

Well over five million tourists visit the broader Arctic every year. Tourists comprise the single greatest human presence in the region, and the majority are marine-based. Passenger vessels made up just under 10% of Arctic maritime activity in 2004; the vast majority of this was for the purpose of tourism, and almost exclusively limited to ice-free waters and the summer months. Most activity was concentrated along the Norwegian coast, where the Hurtigruten line has been operating since 1893. Other areas of high activity include cruises to and around Svalbard, Iceland, the west coast of Greenland and the Aleutian Islands, and the Bering Sea coast of Alaska. Between 2004, when 1.2m cruise-ship passengers visited the Arctic, and 2007, the number of visitors more than doubled.[47] However, while Arctic tourism has been increasing, so has global tourism, which nearly doubled to more than 1bn trips between 1995 and 2012.[48] Arctic tourism comprises less than 1% of the global total.

Arctic tourism is expected to increase as the region warms: not only is access likely to improve, but the real and symbolic importance of the Arctic for global climate change makes it an increasingly attractive destination for many travellers. Simulations of Arctic tourism trends under different emissions scenarios, based purely on projected changes in temperature and precipitation, suggest that the overall numbers of tourists will increase substantially, but there will be little geographical variation from the present pattern.[49]

In economic terms, while tourism and fisheries are both extremely important for the Arctic economy and for the economies of the smaller Arctic nations, they are less significant as a proportion of global activity in their sectors than are energy or mining. Similarly, while smaller sectors, such as satellite communications and undersea telecoms cables, may hold potential for significant relative growth, they will be of marginal importance in absolute terms. The real significance of projected growth in Arctic tourism lies in the chronic environmental impact it will have, and in the increasing capabilities required to both respond to acute environmental threats and for search and rescue (addressed in Chapter Three).

Maritime shipping routes

Convention has it that there are three sea routes in the Arctic: the NWP between the Bering Strait and the Atlantic through the Canadian Archipelago, the NEP – including the NSR – north of Russia, and a Transpolar Passage (TPP) between the Bering Strait and the North Atlantic. It would be a mistake to call these routes 'sea lines of communication' under current climatic conditions, since the TPP is only navigable by heavy icebreakers or submarines and the other two are only open during the summer, and inconsistently at that. Moreover, neither the NWP nor the NSR are single, discrete lanes but rather comprise a multitude of alternative channels with varying ice conditions affecting navigability. As a potential route, the TPP is undefined, will depend on varying ice conditions well into the future, and has several possible channels into the Atlantic. As long as variable ice conditions can require extensive diversion, the Arctic sea routes are in effect broad sea corridors that overlap one another under some conditions, so that between them they comprise the entire Arctic Ocean and adjacent seas.[50]

As part of the 2009 Arctic Marine Shipping Assessment (AMSA), an Arctic Council working group conducted a series of scenario workshops looking at Arctic and regional futures to 2020 and 2050. These used the 2007 IPCC Fourth Assessment Report and the 2004 Arctic Climate Impact Assessment as baselines for projections of climate change in the region; as we noted in Chapter One, these increasingly appear to be conservative. Nearly 120 factors and variables were identified that could shape the future of Arctic marine activity.[51] Twenty were considered most important; they can be grouped under four rubrics:

- *Governance issues*: a stable legal climate; insurance industry engagement; global agreements on construction rules and standards; Arctic maritime enforcement.
- *Geopolitical factors*: the safety of other routes; the escalation of Arctic maritime disputes.
- *Socio-economic factors*: the impact of global weather changes; oil prices; China, Japan and South Korea becoming Arctic maritime nations; transit fees; conflict between indigenous and commercial use; a global shift to nuclear energy; world trade patterns; limited windows of operation.
- *Wild cards*: a major Arctic shipping disaster; rapid climate change; climate change becoming disruptive sooner; the catastrophic loss of the Suez or Panama canals; radical change in global trade dynamics; new resource discoveries.

The assessment concluded that natural-resource development and intra-regional trade, rather than trans-Arctic voyages, are the key drivers of future maritime activity in the region through 2020. The lack of major ports and other critical infrastructure, with the exception of those in Norway and northwest Russia, will be a significant limitation.[52]

Nevertheless, if these passages become consistently open to maritime traffic, even if only seasonally, they could provide significant economic benefits, shortening the distances and transit times between Northern Pacific and European ports. For example, for shipping between Shanghai, the world's busiest container port, and Rotterdam, the NEP route is about 8,716nm, the route via the Suez Canal is 10,547nm, and the route via the Cape of Good Hope is 13,976nm.[53] For most Chinese ports, there is likely to be some reduction in distance. Hong Kong, for example, is the southernmost of China's six ports in the world's busiest top ten. The distance to Rotterdam via the NEP is about 470nm less than via Suez, or 5% of the total. This suggests that for shipping to Europe from any Asian port north of Hong Kong, the Arctic offers potential savings. From Busan, South Korea, to Rotterdam the NEP is 24% shorter than the Suez route, and from Yokohama, Japan, it is 30% shorter. From Vancouver to Rotterdam, the NEP offers distance savings of 21% over the Panama Canal route. For shipping from Pacific ports to Europe, the NWP is equivalent to the NEP, if marginally longer, but for shipping to New York, the savings run between 17% and 24% for the five ports mentioned. The TPP offers even greater savings – up to 39% from Yokohama, 16% from Hong Kong and 28% from Vancouver. Operators could, alternatively, choose to sail more slowly, preserving fuel significantly while arriving at the same time as they would have by following a traditional route. In fact, Arctic conditions are, and likely will remain, such that slower sailing is necessary in any case.

But these distance savings do not automatically translate into savings in time or money. As discussed in Chapter One, the NSR and the NEP were open to commercial traffic in the summer for much of the twentieth century, and in fact even with the newfound interest as the ice cover declines, shipping levels have not yet regained their twentieth-century peak. The short season and harsh conditions impose costs that make even the significantly shorter route economically unappealing under most circumstances. Under conditions of climate change, the season will lengthen until the passage is open year round, but even then operating conditions will remain difficult in comparison to traditional routes, even if coastal infrastructure and search-and-rescue facilities are improved commensurate with the demand from increased traffic. As long as sea ice remains a hazard, for example (and it should be recalled that 'ice-free' can denote up to 15% ice cover in a given area), ships will be forced to choose the safest channels and take diversions, so that the optimum distance savings are unlikely to be achieved. Operating conditions can actually decline with reductions in sea ice, which may increase clouds and fog, and the icing up of vessels. Moreover, climate change will not be linear, and annual variations in conditions will remain considerable. The practicality of Arctic routes as alternatives to traditional shipping lanes is critically dependent on the timing and degree of climate change, both directly and through the effect of uncertainties about future climatic conditions on planning and policy for developing infrastructure.

Another factor limits the utility of the NSR as an alternative to the Suez route between North Pacific ports and Europe. Vessels that can transit the shallow straits between the Laptev and East Siberian seas are limited to a draft of 12.5 metres, a beam of 30 metres, and thus about 50,000 deadweight tonnes (DWT).[54] This is equivalent to the 'Panamax' standard – the size of vessel that can use the Panama Canal – but less than half the capacity of the largest ships that can transit the Suez Canal or the 'New Panamax' standard set by the expansion project due to be completed in 2015. Although the route from East Asia to the US via Suez, for example, is some 5% longer than the Panama route, shipping companies are finding the longer route more economical because of the difference in vessel-size limitations between the two canals.[55] These economic realities will be of significance for any potential expansion of Arctic commercial maritime traffic. The largest commercial ship to transit the NSR was the Russian Suezmax tanker, which took 120,000 tonnes of gas condensate from Norway to Thailand in 2011, but the necessary route north of the New Siberian Islands is not yet reliable and will not be for some time.[56] On the other hand, if global warming opens deep-water routes through the NEP or the TPP appropriate for tankers that are too large to transit Suez, the savings could be extraordinary. Much of the LNG from Norway's Snøhvit field in the Barents Sea is currently shipped 12,500nm to Asia via the Cape of Good Hope, a third as long as the Suez route would be; a northerly NEP route could be nearly 50% shorter, at about 6,500nm.

Thus, it is difficult to calculate potential cost-savings for using an Arctic shipping route over a traditional one. One study compared the costs of the NSR, NWP and TPP over the Suez route from East Asia to Europe for an ice-strengthened general cargo vessel like the German ship that transited the NWP from South Korea to Hamburg in 2009, and for a large container ship.[57] It assumed, for each route, that ice conditions were such that icebreaker escort or support was not required, but insurance costs would be three times the level required for the Suez route (excluding premiums for piracy around the Horn of Africa). For the general cargo vessel sailing from Yokohama to Hamburg, time savings were 11, nine and 12 days for the NEP, NWP and TPP respectively, with corresponding savings of US$200,800, US$178,100 and US$237,000. For the container ship sailing from Shanghai to Hamburg, the figures were three days (US$732,200), one day (US$710,000) and three days (US$876,200) respectively.

The study concluded that, firstly, the impact of insurance costs was negligible compared to that of fuel costs, and that fuel-cost savings and Suez Canal fees made up the bulk of the savings. For the container ship, especially, fuel savings dominated. These were highest (about 50%) for the TPP and lowest (36–39%) for the NWP. For the NEP, the savings for the general cargo ship sailing between Yokohama and Hamburg were 42%, and for the container ship between Shanghai and Hamburg, 40%. Thus, the benefit of the Arctic route depends on fuel price. Using 2002–03 prices, which were relatively low, the savings were about 50% less than for the April 2010 baseline price in the study, while using the peak 2008 price meant savings were about 50% greater. If fuel prices rise in the medium term, as most analysts expect, the savings are potentially greater. But these calculations do not include icebreaker and infrastructure-support fees charged by Russia for use of the NEP. These are currently opaque and negotiable, but if they are set at self-supporting levels, they may offset both the Suez Canal fee and fuel savings, and make the NEP less competitive. Moreover, the calculated fuel savings depend on assumptions about cruising speed, which depends on the presence and amount of sea ice, among other factors. Until the Arctic routes are essentially ice-free, the fuel savings will be lower and the need (and fees) for icebreaker support greater.

Another model-based study, incorporating ice data and based on a single emissions scenario, compared the costs of one variant of the NEP with the Suez route in detail. The chosen variant passes largely north of the Russian 200nm EEZ, avoiding the uncertainty around Russian fee levels, but with ice conditions similar to an NSR variant passing north of the shallower areas. Projections of future container traffic are based on the same economic assumptions and projections that underlie the chosen emissions scenario. The study compared the Suez route to two Arctic fleet-level scenarios: all-year operation of special 'double-acting' vessels, essentially hybrid ships that can operate as icebreakers when going in reverse; and Polar Class 4 container ships that would operate in the Arctic for 100–120 days during summer, and via the Suez route for the remainder of the year. In both cases, the fleets would operate regularly scheduled services. The conclusion was that, under the first scenario, the NSR would not be competitive by 2030, and would only be competitive by 2050 if fuel prices rose to 20% higher than the 2008 peak. Under the second scenario, the NSR would be competitive for traffic from Northeast Asian ports, but not from Hong Kong, by 2030, and possibly for Hong Kong by 2050, if both fuel prices and the length of the summer season were particularly high. The projected volume of trade would involve about 480 large container-ship voyages by 2030, and 850 by 2050, or about 8% and 10% of total container trade between Asia and Europe respectively. Given that these scenarios involve specialised, ice-capable ships, the costs are proportionally greater than those assumed in the first study, but the scenarios would require correspondingly lower infrastructure investment.[58]

A third study has compared the economics of a regular container service by open-water vessels travelling via the Suez route to one by ice-strengthened ships which take the NEP when possible and Suez for the rest of the year.[59] Twenty-seven discrete cases were examined, using Arctic navigation periods of three, six and nine months, with fixed assumptions about the proportion of the route that is ice-free for each; 50%, 85% and 100% reductions in transit fees compared to published levels for 2005; and three levels of fuel prices. The conclusion was that, with current icebreaker fees, the NSR is not economical under any of the fuel-cost or seasonal scenarios. In comparison, the Suez route is economical under the lowest of the three fuel-cost scenarios. (That it is uneconomical with fuel prices near or above the peak 2008 levels is a reflection of the fact that they are assuming comparable ship sizes, but since Suez is capable of taking larger vessels, economies of scale are available.) Reducing icebreaker fees by 50% makes the NSR economical at the lower fuel-price level for the three- and six-month seasons, but not competitive with the Suez route. That longer seasons generate lower profit is counter-intuitive, but stems from the fact that the turnaround and waiting time for ships using the NSR is twice that for those using Suez. Ships using the NSR for three months and Suez the rest of the time can make 11.55 trips per year, versus 11.05 for those using Suez alone. Doubling the Arctic season increases the number of trips by only 6.7%. This increased waiting time is in part due to administrative procedures, and could conceivably be shortened.

With an 85% reduction in fees for the NSR, the Arctic alternative becomes competitive with Suez for a three-month season at the lower fuel-price level, and more profitable than Suez as the season lengthens. For a nine-month Arctic season, it becomes profitable at the price level just below that of the 2008 peak. However, it is only when fees are eliminated entirely that the NSR becomes profitable at a fuel-price level 20% higher than that of 2008, and then only for a nine-month season. At the middle fuel-price level, it is profitable for a six-month season as well. In all cases, with no fees, it is competitive with the Suez route.

All these studies presumed particular routes would be taken. The first quantitative, model-based study of future changes in potential Arctic shipping routes was published in 2013. Lawrence Smith and Scott Stephenson applied their Arctic Transportation Accessibility Model to a range of climate models under two scenarios, looking at the present (2006–15) and mid-century (2040–59).[60] They considered two vessel types: Polar Class 6 (PC6, capable of summer/autumn operation in medium first-year ice, which may include old ice inclusions) and open-water vessels with no hull ice-strengthening.[61] (Russian NSR regulations currently require the equivalent of the PC6 standard. The production and operating costs of such container ships are not significantly higher than those for open-water vessels, but the costs increase exponentially as ice class improves.)[62] They investigated the optimal route for September of each year, defined as the course that minimised total voyage time while avoiding sea ice sufficiently thick or concentrated enough to obstruct the given vessel type. Economic, regulatory and jurisdictional factors were not considered. Using the model retrospectively for 1979–2005 and for current conditions matches the real pattern of limited navigation for the two vessel types restricted to the NEP/NSR; for open-water ships, this involves routes between Franz Josef Land and Novaya Zemlya and through the straits separating Severnaya Zemlya, the New Siberian Islands and Wrangel Island from the Russian mainland. Optimal available routes for PC6 vessels pass north of Svalbard, Franz Josef Land and the other islands but for the most part remain within Russia's 200nm EEZ and well away from the pole. For 2040–59, availability of routes for open-water vessels to transit the NSR both increases in frequency and expands northwards from the Russian coast, closely mimicking the present pattern for PC6 vessels for the more conservative emissions scenario. For the more extreme scenario the range of optimal routes is greater, with some approaching the pole. In both cases, the NPP and the NWP are fully open for both vessel classes. These projections are for September only, but as optimal routes expand in frequency and geographically for the period of minimum sea ice, the length of the available sailing season will increase; the current optimal September routes through the NEP will be open for much longer, perhaps quadrupling from 30 to 120 days by mid-century.[63]

Conclusions

Although there are commercial opportunities in the Arctic, they are not necessarily as lucrative or revolutionary as the prevailing popular narrative would suggest. Given the large number of unknowns, it is impossible to project the timing and degree to which Arctic maritime shipping routes will become globally significant and competitive with the present alternatives. That they will do so at all is not inevitable, even as the sea ice progressively declines. Critical economic drivers such as fuel costs, and politically driven factors such as user fees for the NSR and investments in coastal infrastructure, search-and-rescue capabilities, and new icebreakers will be important. Shipping between Arctic ports and bulk shipping from the Arctic to non-Arctic destinations, especially of hydrocarbons, are likely to see the greatest and earliest increases. Trans-Arctic shipping is likely to see much slower growth, especially for container vessels. Moreover, if fuel prices rise significantly, making trans-Arctic shipping more attractive, it will also make Arctic hydrocarbon production attractive, and thus increase related shipping. By mid-century, it is likely that both intra- and trans-Arctic maritime activity will be at least an order of magnitude greater than at present.

The Arctic already provides 10% of global oil production and 25% of global gas production, roughly comparable to the USGS's best estimates of the Arctic's share of the world's remaining undiscovered hydrocarbon resources. The great uncertainty in those estimates – a 90% chance that the region contains 6–23% of undiscovered oil and 14–54% of undiscovered gas – does not rule out the possibility that the Arctic might become more important globally as a source of energy, but it is equally possible that its relative significance will in fact decline. The same is true for other mineral resources, notably the rare earths. Particularly difficult operating conditions, remoteness of resources and strict environmental regulations all increase the costs of exploiting resources in the High North, while the economic viability of mining and maritime trade routes will depend on factors such as international prices for minerals, the availability of new conventional and unconventional resources elsewhere on the globe and possible charges for infrastructural use along the NSR. Investment in infrastructure to support newly or increasingly accessible maritime shipping routes will in turn depend on the level of activity expected from the development of new resources, as well as on the degree to which the distance savings offered by Arctic transit routes are offset by comparatively greater operating and insurance costs due to the harsh conditions; restrictions on draft and tonnage of vessels; short operating seasons; the rate of sea-ice decline; and other factors.

But even relatively modest and incremental opportunities for economic development and exploitation of Arctic routes and resources mean that Arctic states are placing increasing strategic importance on the region. The next chapter analyses the history and development of the Arctic as a strategic space; whether this new focus comprises a 'militarisation' of the Arctic with the potential to ignite an arms race, leading to a crisis, confrontation and other dangerous consequences; and the potential for military cooperation and the development of an international security architecture for the High North.

Notes

[1] Dmitry Bogoyavlenskiy and Andy Siggner, 'Arctic Demography', in *Arctic Human Development Report* (Akureyri: Stefansson Arctic Institute, 2004), p. 27; Arctic Council, Sustainable Development Working Group, 'Report on Arctic Energy', 2009, p. 7, http://library.arcticportal.org/1531/1/SDWG_ArcticEnergyReport_2009.pdf.

[2] USGS, 'Circum-Arctic Resource Appraisal: estimates of undiscovered oil and gas north of the Arctic Circle', May 2008, http://pubs.usgs.gov/fs/2008/3049/; Donald L. Gautier et al., 'Assessment of undiscovered oil and gas in the Arctic', *Science*, vol. 325, no. 5,391, 29 May 2009, pp. 1175–9.

[3] Philip Budzik, 'Arctic Oil and Gas Potential', US Energy Information Administration, Working Paper, October 2009, http://www.arlis.org/docs/vol1/AlaskaGas/Paper/Paper_EIA_2009_ArcticOilGasPotential.pdf.

[4] *Arctic Oil and Gas 2007* (Oslo: AMAP, 2007), vol. 1, ch. 2, p. 4.

[5] *Ibid.*

[6] USGS, 'Circum-Arctic Resource Appraisal'; Gautier et al., 'Assessment of undiscovered oil and gas in the Arctic'.

[7] Infield Systems, 'Offshore Arctic Oil and Gas Market Report to 2018', 2012, http://www.infield.com/market-forecast-reports/offshore-arctic-frontiers-market-report.

[8] Gautier et al., 'Assessment of undiscovered oil and gas in the Arctic'.

[9] *Arctic Oil and Gas 2007*, ch. 2, p. 253; Solveig Glomsrød and Iulie Aslaksen (eds), 'The Economy of the North' 2008', *Statistics Analyses*,

Statistics Norway, November 2009, p. 29; USGS, 'World Petroleum Assessment 2000 – Description and Results', http://pubs.usgs.gov/dds/dds-060/.

10 Christopher J. Schenk, 'Geology and petroleum potential of the West Greenland–East Canada Province', Geological Society Memoir, no. 35, 2011, pp. 627–45, http://pubs.er.usgs.gov/publication/70036499.

11 USGS, 'Circum-Arctic Resource Appraisal'; USGS, 'Assessment of Undiscovered Oil and Gas Resources of the West Siberian Basin Province, Russia, 2010', June 2011, http://pubs.usgs.gov/fs/2011/3050/.

12 For a detailed survey of the current state of Arctic energy exploration and development, see Jerry Greenberg, 'Regional report: the Arctic', World Oil, vol. 233, no. 11, November 2012, http://www.worldoil.com/November-2012-Regional-Report-The-Arctic.html; for prospects over the short term, see Infield Systems, 'Offshore Arctic Oil and Gas Market Report to 2018'.

13 Budzik, 'Arctic Oil and Gas Potential'; Willy Østreng et al., Shipping in Arctic Waters: A Comparison of the Northeast, Northwest and Trans Polar Passages (Berlin: Springer, 2013), pp. 103–4; Arctic Oil and Gas 2007, ch. 2, p. 12.

14 Infield Systems, 'Offshore Arctic Oil and Gas Market Report to 2018'.

15 Arctic Oil and Gas 2007, ch. 2, p. 252.

16 Budzik, 'Arctic Oil and Gas Potential', p. 9.

17 Glomsrød and Aslaksen (eds), 'The Economy of the North 2008 ', pp. 71–3, http://www.ssb.no/a/english/publikasjoner/pdf/sa112_en/sa112_en.pdf.

18 Scott R. Stephenson, Laurence C. Smith and John A. Agnew, 'Divergent long-term trajectories of human access to the Arctic', Nature Climate Change, vol. 1, 2011, pp. 156–60.

19 AMAP, 'Arctic Climate Issues 2011: Changes in Arctic Snow, Water, Ice and Permafrost', SWIPA 2011 Overview Report, pp. 69–73.

20 Ernest Wong, 'Geopolitics of Arctic Oil and Gas: the Dwindling Relevance of Territorial Claims', New Voices in Public Policy, vol. 7, Spring 2013.

21 The White House, 'National Strategy for the Arctic Region', May 2013, http://www.whitehouse.gov/sites/default/files/docs/nat_arctic_strategy.pdf.

22 Figures for this section are derived from Glomsrød and Aslaksen (eds), 'The Economy of the North 2008', pp. 37–66; and Østreng et al., Shipping in Arctic Waters: A Comparison of the Northeast, Northwest and Trans Polar Passages, pp. 105 7. The figures are subject to the caveats discussed in the previous paragraph.

23 Østreng et al., Shipping in Arctic Waters, pp. 105–7.

24 Glomsrød and Aslaksen (eds), 'The Economy of the North'.

25 World Oil and Gas Review 2010 (Rome: ENI, 2010), pp. 10, 48; F.W. Wellmer and J.D. Becker-Platen, 'Sustainable development and the exploitation of mineral and energy resources: a review', International Journal of Earth Sciences, vol. 91, 2002, pp. 723–45, http://bscw-app1.ethz.ch/pub/bscw.cgi/d168015/Wellmer_Becker%20Platen_2002.pdf.

26 AMAP, 'Arctic Climate Issues 2011', p. 67.

27 USGS, 'Rare earth elements – critical resources for high technology', 2002, http://geopubs. wr.usgs.gov/fact-sheet/fs087-02/. For a breakdown of usage by element and application, see Keith R. Long et al., *The Principal Rare Earth Elements Deposits of the United States – A Summary of Domestic Deposits and a Global Perspective* (Reston, VA: US Geological Survey, 2010), p. 13, http://pubs.usgs.gov/ sir/2010/5220/.

28 *Ibid.*, p. 15.

29 *Ibid.*, p. 13.

30 *Ibid*, p. 11.

31 Keith Bradsher, 'China is blocking minerals, executives say', *New York Times,* 23 September 2010, http://www.nytimes. com/2010/09/24/business/energy-environment/24mineral.html.

32 Long et al., *The Principal Rare Earth Elements Deposits of the United States,* pp. 18–20.

33 Molycorp, 'Year in Review: 2012', http://www.molycorp.com/ wp-content/uploads/Molycorp-Year-End-Reivew-2012.pdf.

34 MIT, 'Mission 2016: The Future of Strategic Natural Resources' website, 'Rare earth elements supply and demand'.

35 Greenland Minerals and Energy, 'Fact Sheet', 2012, http://www.ggg. gl/docs/fact-sheets/GMEL_Fact_ Sheet_2012.pdf; Molycorp, *Year in Review: 2012.*

36 Greenland Minerals and Energy, 'Kvanefjeld feasibility study developments: mine and concentrator study lowers initial start-up costs', 26 March 2013, http://www.ggg.gl/docs/ ASX-announcements/Mine-and-Concentrator-study.pdf.

37 MIT, 'Mission 2016: The Future of Strategic Natural Resources' website, 'Rare earth elements supply and demand'.

38 *Ibid.*

39 Long et al., *The Principal Rare Earth Elements Deposits of the United States,* pp. 19–23.

40 Greenland Minerals and Energy, 'Fact Sheet', 2012.

41 'Arctic Opening: Opportunity and risk in the High North', Lloyds and Chatham House, 2012.

42 AMAP, 'Arctic Climate Impact Assessment', 2005, pp. 770–1.

43 *Ibid.* For an up-to-date assessment of current trends, see Conservation of Arctic Flora and Fauna Working Group, Arctic Council, *Arctic Biodiversity Assessment: Status and trends in Arctic biodiversity* (Akureyri: CAFF, 2013), http:// www.arcticbiodiversity.is./, pp. 378–411.

44 Gérard Duhaime, 'Economic systems', in *Arctic Human Development Report* (Akureyri: Stefansson Arctic Institute, 2004), pp. 72-3.

45 AMAP, 'Arctic Climate Impact Assessment', pp. 809–12.

46 *Ibid.*, p. 854; Conservation of Arctic Flora and Fauna Working Group, Arctic Council, *Arctic Biodiversity Assessment*, p. 277.

47 C. Michael Hall and Jarkko Sararinen, 'Polar Tourism: Definitions and Dimensions', *Scandinavian Journal of Hospitality and Tourism*, vol. 10, no. 4, 2010, pp. 448–67; Arctic Council, 'Arctic Marine Shipping Assessment 2009 Report', pp. 78, 99.

48 UN World Tourism Organization, 'UNWTO Tourism Highlights 2013 Edition', p. 2.

49 Richard S.J. Tol and Sharon Walsh, 'Climate Change and Tourism in the Arctic Circle', University of Sussex ,Department of Economics Working Paper no. 5212, 2012, http://www.sussex.ac.uk/economics/documents/wps-52-2012.pdf.

50 Østreng, et al., *Shipping in Arctic Waters*.

51 Arctic Council, 'Arctic Marine Shipping Assessment 2009 Report', p. 93.

52 *Ibid.*, p. 5.

53 Distances given in this book are calculated using the tables in National Geospatial-Intelligence Agency, *Distances Between Ports*, Publication 151, (Bethesda, MD: USGPO, 2001). For the NSR, we take the distance from Pacific ports to Nome, Alaska, then through the NSR to Pevek, Tiksi, Chelyuskin and Murmansk. For through traffic, and given the right ice conditions, the route might be as much as 500nm shorter, making the savings even more significant. For the TPP, we use a figure of 2,300nm for the distance from Nome to Svalbard, following Østreng et al., *Shipping in Arctic Waters*, p. 348. For the NWP, we use Østreng and colleagues' figure of 3,000nm from the Bering Strait to the Davis Strait. Our figures differ, usually by less than one percentage point, from other published distances, but these are usually presented without explanation or citation and it is often difficult to determine how they have been calculated. For information on container-traffic volumes, see World Shipping Council, 'Top 50 World Container Ports', http://www.worldshipping.org/about-the-industry/global-trade/top-50-world-container-ports.

54 Malte Humpert and Andreas Raspotnik, 'The Future of Arctic Shipping', *Port Technology International*, no. 55, Summer 2012, pp. 10–11, http://issuu.com/henleymedia/docs/pti55/1.

55 Kyunghee Park, 'Maersk Line to Dump Panama Canal for Suez as Ships Get Bigger', Bloomberg, 11 March 2013.

56 'Arctic Transit: Northern Sea Route', *Insight*, no. 4, March 2012, pp. 4–6, http://www.lr.org/Images/Insight%20issue%204%20Mar%202012_tcm155-236296.pdf.

57 Østreng, et al., *Shipping in Arctic Waters*, pp. 340–53.

58 Lars Ingolf Eide, Magnus Eide and Øyvind Endresen, 'Shipping across the Arctic Ocean: A feasible option in 2030–2050 as a result of global warming?', Research and Innovation Position Paper 04-2010 (Høvik: Det Norske Veritas, 2010).

59 Miaojia Liu and Jacob Kronbak, 'The potential economic viability of using the Northern Sea Route (NSR) as an alternative route between Asia and Europe', *Journal of Transport Geography*, vol. 18, 2010, pp. 434–44.

60 Lawrence C. Smith and Scott R. Stephenson, 'New Trans-Arctic shipping routes navigable by mid-century', *Proceedings of the National Academy of Sciences of the United States of America*, 27 February 2013, http://www.pnas.org/content/early/2013/02/27/1214212110.full.pdf.

61 International Maritime Organization, 'Guidelines for Ships Operating in Arctic Ice Covered Waters', 23 December 2002.

62 Robert E. Dvorak, *Engineering and Economic Implications of Ice-Classed Containerships*, MIT, June 2009.

63 Humpert and Raspotnik, 'The Future of Arctic Shipping', pp. 10–11.

CHAPTER THREE

The Arctic as a theatre of military operations

Even with all the caveats, it is clear that the potential economic benefits to be gained from the Arctic are substantial. The likely shift in global maritime trade routes and the presence of hydrocarbons and other resources confirm the strategic value of the region.

Yet where there is strategic value, there is often competition, as jealous nations attempt to secure the resources and profits that such regions can produce. Moreover, despite the formal legal framework provided by UNCLOS, the warming of the region has created a new, essentially ungoverned space in the Arctic Ocean that governments are eager to secure. The situation is further complicated by territorial disputes such as those over Hans Island and the US–Canadian border in the Beaufort Sea.

It is in this context that military activity and presence in the Arctic have increased, furthering the popular narrative of regional competition and rivalry. The reality is somewhat more complex. While such a narrative has been reinforced by occasionally belligerent rhetoric and an increase in military deployments, there have also been conflicting messages from politicians and a series of cooperative exercises. Military activity has certainly increased recently but it has been from a historically low base and, in most cases, pales in comparison to the levels of activity in the Cold War. The Arctic is therefore a new space for greater operations that will result in an increased military presence; but this does not necessarily suggest impending conflict. In fact, there is the possibility that the Arctic could become a region character-ised by unusual military cooperation rather than competition.

The Arctic as a strategic space

Although seasonal sea-ice decline has emphasised the potential strategic importance of the High North, in reality the region has been of military interest for more than a century.

Initially, the Arctic was seen as a barrier rather than a conduit, given the grave difficulties in transiting significant military supplies through the region. Moreover, the lack of population centres left little for aggressive explorers to gain from activity in the Arctic.

Although the often militant Vikings explored Iceland, Greenland and the north of the Scandinavian peninsula to reach the White Sea as early as the ninth century, much of this activ-ity involved settlement or peaceful exploration. Subsequently, however, conflict among the Scandinavian tribes and countries, and other northern European states occurred frequently as expanding nations came into conflict. The Treaty of Nöteborg in 1323 and the Treaty of Novgorod in 1326 settled the Swedish– and Norwegian–Novgorodian borders respectively. The northernmost fortress in the world dates from this period: Vardøhus Fortress was constructed in the fourteenth century in what is now Finnmark, during skirmishes between Norway and the Novgorodian tributary Karelia.

From the sixteenth century onwards, conflict among the newly emergent nation-states of northern Europe and Russia became more intense, particularly as the Swedish Empire rose and its power was contested. However, much of the actual conflict occurred in the sub-Arctic Baltic region, with little activity in the far north. The most northerly campaign of the Great Northern War, for instance, led to action on the northern coast of the Gulf of Bothnia in Lapland's Tornio, just south of the Arctic Circle.

The economic benefits of trade to some Arctic towns made them of greater strategic value to extra-regional powers in subsequent wars. During the Napoleonic wars, the Royal Navy raided the Finnmark towns of Hasvik and Hammerfest, seeking to disrupt the Pomor trade (between northwestern Russia and northern Norway) and expand a blockade that already encompassed France and her allies. HMS *Nyaden*, captured from the Royal Dano-Norwegian Navy, engaged in small actions in the Barents Sea and the Kola Peninsula during these years. Later in the century, a three-ship squadron of the Royal Navy operated in the White Sea and bombarded the Arctic town of Kola and the sub-Arctic Solovetsky Islands during the Crimean War.

By the early twentieth century, the Arctic was an area of keen exploration, often by naval personnel. But it remained inaccessible for large-scale military activity and more a hindrance than an opportunity for interested countries. Russia found this to its cost during the 1904–05 Russo-Japanese War. With the Russian Far East Fleet besieged in Port Arthur, Moscow decided to reinforce its position by sailing the lion's share of its Baltic Fleet eastwards. Had the NSR been open, the journey could have been made in as little as three months. As it was, the fleet was forced to sail around Europe, the African continent and Cape of Good Hope. This was owing to British support for the Japanese and London's refusal to allow the Russian ships access to the Suez Canal, following the killing of three British fishermen by Russians in the Dogger Bank incident. The 28 warships of the Baltic Fleet therefore had to travel nearly 30,000km to reinforce the Far East Fleet, in a voyage lasting nine months. (The flotilla, renamed the Second Pacific Squadron, had barely entered the theatre of operations when its beleaguered and exhausted crew had to fight the Battle of Tsushima; the result was an absolute victory for Japan.)

The impassability of the Arctic during the Russo-Japanese War encouraged Moscow to reconsider whether the NSR might be a viable passage after all, and equally to militarise areas of the Arctic to protect northern trade routes. A five-year hydrographic expedition (1910–15) to survey the entire NSR, involving two purpose-built icebreakers, was followed by the establishment of Murmansk as a port for military supplies during the First World War.[1] As part of the transformation of Murmansk, the precursor to the Northern Fleet was created in 1916 when the Arctic Sea Flotilla was established, but it was short-lived, falling to the White Russians during the revolution. The ensuing Russian civil war also saw Allied forces occupy Murmansk and Arkhangelsk in order to assist the Czechoslovak Legions and secure military supplies that were trapped in Murmansk following the revolution. The Royal Navy also sustained a flotilla in the Baltic Sea until 1921 in a bid to support the White Russians and Baltic independence. Following Russia's Arctic Sea Flotilla, the White Sea Flotilla was created in 1920, although it was disbanded in 1923. It was not until 1933 that the Northern Flotilla was created and deployed to Polyarny, eventually becoming the Northern Fleet in 1937.

The pre-war modern period therefore saw little conflict in the High North, but a realisation that the region had strategic value in the first half of the twentieth century led to a gradual militarisation of the Russian Arctic. This was most likely owing to technological advances that made it easier to travel to and communicate with the region, thus allowing for commercial trade and military activity.

The growing strategic importance of the Arctic was recognised publicly in 1935 by US Army General Billy Mitchell, who stated in Congress that 'in the future, whoever holds Alaska will hold the world … I think it is the most strategic place in the world.'[2] It was during the Second World War, however, that the Arctic, from a strategic perspective, came into its own. After the outbreak of war in 1939, France and Britain made plans for the mining of Norwegian territorial waters, and even an occupation of Narvik and the Swedish Arctic iron region, to prevent the export of ore to Germany. A secondary objective soon arose: opening a route for assistance to Finland after it was attacked by the Soviet Union.

Adolf Hitler's invasion and occupation of Norway in 1940 was essentially pre-emptive, to forestall the Allied interdiction of Swedish iron, but the Norwegian Arctic became an important basing area for German air and naval forces operating against Allied convoys to Murmansk and the White Sea.[3] Those convoys successfully delivered nearly 4 million tonnes of supplies over the course of the war, with the Royal Navy-protected Arctic convoys being a key reason for the Soviet Union's eventual success in resisting German advances. More than twice as many supplies were delivered across the Pacific to Siberian ports, and about 5% of this was transported over at least part of the NSR, while German U-boats and cruisers operated in the Barents and Kara seas. Many North Atlantic convoys were also routed through Arctic waters (under the AMAP/AHDR definition) to take advantage of air cover from bases in Newfoundland and Iceland. Those bases, as well as several in Greenland, were also important for the transport of aircraft to the European theatre. Thousands of aircraft and selected essential supplies were also sent via an Alaska–Siberia air route in order to keep the Soviets well stocked with materiel. Among these supplies were materials critical to the Soviet atomic-bomb programme.[4]

Beyond the Arctic patrols, a variety of areas in the High North witnessed different actions during the Second World War. The Winter War between Finland and the Soviet Union in 1939–40 demonstrated the difficulties of operating in the harsh conditions of northern Europe in winter, and included the advance of the Soviet 14th Army from Murmansk to capture the Arctic port of Petsamo, and from there to Rovaniemi. For its part, the Soviet Union agreed to allow four armed German merchant cruisers through the NSR to attack British shipping in the Pacific; in the event, only one was sent, escorted by Russian icebreakers.[5] The *Komet*, a German cruiser, was the first warship to use the NSR when it transited from Germany to the Pacific in 1940.[6] The Pacific was also the scene of a rare occupation of US territory by a foreign power: in 1942, the Japanese sent a small expeditionary force to occupy Attu and Kiska islands in the Aleutian Islands. The occupation lasted a year, given US priorities elsewhere in the Pacific and the difficulty of operations in such northern climes during the winter.

The Arctic also provided useful meteorological data for military operations. Germany briefly established weather stations on Spitsbergen and Jan Mayen, and between 1941 and 1944 established a series of temporary stations on the east coast of Greenland. Data from Allied Arctic weather stations was critical in the success of the 1944 D-Day landings in France.

The Arctic retained its strategic importance during the Cold War. The shortest route between the Soviet Union and the continental United States for aircraft and ballistic missiles was over the polar region. The Arctic was thus an important theatre for strategic air defence, early warning and potentially ballistic-missile defence. The Distant Early Warning (DEW) Line was a string of early-warning radar stations constructed by the US and Canada across the entire far north of the continent and along the Aleutian and Faroe islands, as well as Greenland and Iceland. The construction project was a feat of transportation and engineering, with 63 stations completed across Alaska and Canada in three years, often in punishing Arctic winter conditions. Nuclear-powered ballistic-missile submarines (SSBNs), an important component of the strategic deterrent for both sides, could use the sea ice to hide and as cover against anti-submarine warfare, and Soviet strategic bomber bases were also located in the Arctic. Much hydrographic and bathymetric research was therefore classified. A substantial proportion of Soviet naval forces in all categories – strategic and attack submarines; naval aircraft; capital ships; and coastal-defence and escort vessels – were based on the Kola Peninsula. They posed a strategic threat to NATO's transatlantic sea lines of communication via the Norwegian and Greenland seas and the Greenland–Iceland–UK gap, making the defence of this region critical for the Allies and providing a key role for the Royal Navy.

Russian submarine activity throughout the Arctic was a concern not only for the US during the Cold War, but also for Scandinavian countries that on occasion saw Russian submarines approach major population centres. In 1981, for example, a Soviet *Whiskey*-class submarine ran aground in Gåsefjärden, Sweden, and the 1982 Håsfjärden incident involved an intense hunt in the Stockholm archipelago for what was believed to be a Soviet submarine.[7]

Conversely, protection of the Soviet strategic deterrent and homeland required an ability to prevent the Allies from approaching through these waters in the other direction, and a substantial number of Soviet naval exercises in the region were strategically defensive in nature.[8] The Soviets conducted about a third of their nuclear tests on Novaya Zemlya between 1955 and 1990.

Russia's northern front

In the post-Cold War environment, overall activity and presence in the Arctic was reduced. The peace dividend of the 1990s led to declining defence expenditure among all eight Arctic nations, with some of the starkest decreases in Russia. According to *The Military Balance*, the official Russian defence budget declined from US$133.7 billion to just US$7.5bn in this period.[9] A lack of funding meant that vessels, submarines and aircraft of the

Northern Fleet were not maintained, and lacked the resources and staff to ensure regular patrols. The number of patrols by Northern Fleet nuclear-powered submarines, for example, fell from 80 per year in 1985 to 18 in 1995, and the number of total submarine patrols from 230 in 1984 to fewer than ten in the early 2000s. In 2002, no ballistic-missile submarine patrols occurred at all.[10]

This situation began to reverse later in the 2000s, as Russian economic growth dramatically improved amid a resources boom. In 1999, the Russian defence budget increased in real terms for the first time since the end of the Cold War, and it has continued to grow since, reaching US$86.7bn (measured by purchasing power parity) in 2011. Its defence budget was the fourth-largest in the world in 2012.[11]

The growth in Russian defence spending has been accompanied by concomitant increases in naval procurement. Programmes are currently in place for the ongoing procurement of *Borey*-class ballistic-missile submarines; *Yasen*-class nuclear-powered submarines; *Lada*- and improved *Kilo*-class diesel-electric submarines; *Gepard*-, *Steregushchi*-, *Admiral Gorshkov*- and *Admiral Grigorovich*-class frigates; and *Buyan*- and *Buyan*-M-class corvettes. Most substantially, Russia has also signed a contract for the provision of two *Mistral*-class amphibious-assault vessels, with the likely future procurement of two more, from France. The *Mistral* is a powerful ship that will be the second-largest in the Russian fleet, behind the solitary *Kuznetsov*-class aircraft carrier, and can carry 16 heavy helicopters.

These various programmes, although often severely delayed and facing various other problems in their delivery, are nonetheless transforming the Russian fleet, which had essentially atrophied and decayed since the late 1980s. In fact, in the two decades following the end of the Cold War in 1991, Russia only commissioned 11 new surface combatants (from patrol craft to destroyers).

Russian ambitions do not stop there, however. The latest iteration of the State Armaments Programme, a quinquennial publication laying out the government's ten-year procurement plans, was published in 2011 and looked forward to 2020. According to this document, Moscow intends to spend US$132bn on naval procurement. Whether or not this spending figure will be reached is questionable, as previous such figures have proven too ambitious to fulfil. Russia is also infamous for its loss of funding to corruption, with the Audit Chamber estimating that US$3.9bn was lost in this way in 2012.[12]

Nonetheless, Russia clearly is pursuing a concerted, and to some extent more realistic, policy to recapitalise its fleet. The State Armaments Programme 2020 particularly focuses on the procurement of frigates and submarines, the workhorses of the navy that allow Moscow to better secure its near-seas. There is currently no destroyer, cruiser or aircraft carrier in build, and it appears that the carrier programme in particular has been delayed until the navy as a whole is in a better shape.

Within this general recapitalisation of the navy, priorities are spread across the five naval organisations. Yet the more realistic focus on smaller combatants means that fleets other than the Northern Fleet are currently benefitting the most. Diesel-electric submarines are being purchased for the Black Sea Fleet (BSF), for instance, while the new frigates are intended to head for the Baltic and Pacific fleets, as well as the BSF and the Caspian flotilla. Corvettes are also expected to head for the Caspian. The first *Mistral* will be deployed to the Pacific.

This shift in focus away from the Northern Fleet towards the smaller organisations reflects a change in Russia's strategic posture as it prioritises its Asian commitments, tries to secure its southern borders and sees NATO as less of a threat. The Northern Fleet, however, is not being entirely abandoned. Based in Severomorsk and along the Kola Peninsula and White Sea, the fleet continues to be the base for Russia's largest vessels and has been the most substantial of Russia's five naval organisations; it is home to just under two-thirds of the country's submarine fleet, including three-quarters of the currently operational SSBN fleet.[13]

While it has seen sizeable reductions in its capacity since the Cold War, Russia is now making a concerted effort to rebuild, or at least rejuvenate, its presence in the north. The first new SSBN in more than 20 years, the *Yuri Dolgoruky*, entered the Northern Fleet in January 2013, with more to follow in the *Borey* class. The 200th Motor Rifle Brigade in Pechenga will form the base of a new Arctic brigade that will be established within the Northern Fleet by 2015. Airfields that have been abandoned since the fall of the Soviet Union may be brought back into operation, while a squadron of MiG-31s will be deployed to Rogachevo on the island of Novaya Zemlya in Arkhangelsk oblast by the end of 2013.[14] Most recently, President Vladimir Putin announced the planned reopening of the Cold War-era naval and air base on the Novosibirsk Islands. The announcement was accompanied by a high-profile form of naval diplomacy, with a ten-ship flotilla arriving in the islands, led by the flagship of the Northern Fleet, *Pyotr Veliky* (Peter the Great). Interestingly, despite the flotilla arriving in September, they were accompanied by four nuclear icebreakers, demonstrating the difficulties of operating in the High North.[15]

Russian activity in the Arctic has also increased. In August 2007, Moscow renewed long-range aviation patrols to the Atlantic and the Pacific, and over the Arctic, oceans. Strategic bomber flights along the Norwegian coast increased from just 14 in 2006 to 97 in 2008; although the number declined in subsequent years, it rose to over 55 in 2012.[16] In March 2013, two Tu-22M3 *Backfire* bombers and four Su-27 multi-role aircraft flew within 20 miles of Sweden's borders; the failure of the Swedish Air Force to scramble in response to the night-time exercises led to searing media criticism.[17] Surface naval patrols also returned to Arctic waters for the first time since the fall of the Soviet Union in 2008.[18]

The Russian military has therefore recovered somewhat from the dire circumstances of the post-Cold War environment, but it is equally struggling to deal with the legacy of a lack of investment in its equipment. The recapitalisation of its fleet is on the surface a concern for neighbouring states, but it is occurring from a very low base of capability. Equally, the focus on smaller vessels will, for the foreseeable future, benefit organisations beyond the Northern Fleet. In line with this military rejuvenation, Moscow has touted the need to increase its military presence in the Arctic, but the force posture announced thus far is modest. The primary change in the next few years will be a renovation of the SSBN fleet, a factor that underlines the strategic importance of the Arctic but does not suggest state-based military competition in the region on a significant scale. It seems, therefore, presumptive to call the Russian defence modernisation a militarisation of the Arctic, particularly as current activity remains a shadow of that seen in the Cold-War era.

Nordic cooperation

In light of Russia's defence improvements generally and a modest increase in its Arctic presence and activity, it is natural that Nordic countries are concerned. This concern has been exacerbated by a perception of a reassertive Moscow following the 2007 cyber attacks against Estonia, in which Russia was implicated, and the 2008 Russo-Georgian war.

Yet the Nordic countries have been stymied by austerity since the late 2000s, and, prior to that, by an unwillingness to invest in the defence sector, given the post-Cold War peace dividend. Defence spending as a percentage of GDP declined in all of the Nordic countries between 1991 and 2011, with quite dramatic decreases in Norway (from 3.3% to 1.4%) and Sweden (from 2.5% to 1.1%).[19] This situation is not set to change in most of the Nordic countries: in 2013, all but Norway saw their defence budgets decline.[20] Denmark is not expected to witness any nominal growth in its defence budget until 2015.

This has not stopped some significant procurement projects from going forward, some of which are directly tied to the Arctic or seem to suggest state-based military procurement competition. Norway, less constrained by the global financial crisis since 2008, given its resource wealth, has been the most active Nordic country in modernising its military. Norway's five *Fridtjof Nansen*-class frigates – the last of which was commissioned in 2011 – have introduced a substantially more capable surface combatant to the navy, supported by six fast and stealthy *Skjold*-class patrol craft. Together, these two classes have greatly improved Norway's ability to defend its coastline, although neither class of vessel is ice-capable. It is not only in the naval sphere that Norway is investing in its defence procurement: US$880m has been set aside for the purchase of the first batch of 52 F-35 Joint Strike Fighters, to be delivered from 2013. The importance of the High North to Oslo was also reflected in its decision to relocate the National Joint Headquarters from Jåttå in southern Norway to Bodø in the north during August 2009. This move followed the 2008 defence-policy paper that affirmed that 'the northern regions are Norway's prime area for strategic investment', indicating Oslo's increased interest in the Arctic.[21]

Denmark, too, has embarked on its largest procurement programme to date with its three *Iver Huitfeldt*-class frigates. While these vessels are not ice-capable, they are significant purchases; of more direct relevance to the Arctic, though, are the two *Knud Rasmussen*-class patrol vessels commissioned in 2008 and 2009, and the four *Thetis*-class frigates commissioned in the early 1990s. While neither class of vessel is armed with anti-ship missiles, they are both built to operate in first-year ice. Copenhagen's focus on the High North was also exemplified by the formation of a joint Arctic Command in October 2012, based in Nuuk, Greenland. Finland is currently engaged in a US$800m investment in its air-defence system, to install the Kongsberg/ Raytheon NASAMS II to replace the current Buk (SA-11) *Gadfly* system. Sweden, meanwhile, is seeking to purchase between 40 and 60 *Gripens* NG, in a partnership deal with Switzerland, which is seeking to purchase 22 units.

These capabilities appear designed to cope with state-based threats, rather than the asymmetric, non-state actors a government might be concerned with for maritime security operations. This would suggest a general armament in order to hedge against possible state-based conflict. However, it is also the case that some of these procurements may not be targeted towards the Arctic specifically; arguably, the *Fridtjof Nansen* class was built to allow Norway a greater ability to deploy overseas, with the lead vessel's first deployment being to the Gulf of Aden on counter-piracy missions. In addition, these procurements are insufficient to maintain the levels of armament seen during the Cold War. Norway's number of armed-services personnel has fallen from more than 32,000 in 1992 to fewer than 24,500 in 2012 (reserves have seen even larger decreases, from 285,000 troops to 45,000). Denmark has similarly seen a decrease in personnel, from 29,200 to 16,500; Finland has seen its force, which is largely reliant on conscripts, reduced from 27,300 to 16,000; and Sweden has seen its personnel fall sharply from 60,500 to 20,500. While troop numbers do not equate to capability, the reductions in personnel demonstrate the difficulties in maintaining a permanent presence throughout the Nordic countries, and in particular in the frozen climes of the Arctic. There has been a gradual move northwards in the basing of some troops and equipment in recent years, but in reality the Arctic presence is very small in most Nordic countries. Denmark's Arctic Command comprises a small headquarters in Nuuk and a rotational presence of naval vessels. Norway maintains the largest Arctic presence, consisting of several army battalions.

The overall downward trend in defence spending and an inability to maintain previous levels of readiness and armament have encouraged wider coordination among the ministries of defence of the Nordic countries. Such defence cooperation has existed since the 1960s in peace-support operations, but gathered momentum in the 1990s as the peace dividend encouraged closer coordination. A Nordic-specific coordination mechanism is seen as viable, given the close political ties between the countries, some shared cultural-linguistic links and economic similarities. Moreover, as the various nations are not universally members of the two major multilateral organisations in Western Europe, NATO and the EU, a Nordic defence mechanism allows the various states to coordinate outside of these structures. Norway, Denmark and Iceland have been members of NATO since its inception in 1949 (Finland and Sweden are members of the Partnerships for Peace programme); and Denmark, Finland and Sweden are members of the EU (Iceland is in formal negotiations to join but its application has been suspended, pending a referendum).

Key within this closer Nordic coordination has been NORDEFCO, the Nordic Defence Cooperation organisation. Founded in 2009, the organisation aims to build capability development in a coordinated fashion within the region, including through joint procurement, pooling and sharing of capabilities, and cooperation in training, exercises, human-resource development and strategy. NORDEFCO follows and supersedes previous Nordic defence cooperation agreements, including the Nordic Coordinated Arrangement for Military Peace Support (NORDCAPS); the procurement cooperation, NORDAC; and NORDSUP, led by the chiefs of defence. NORDEFCO has subsumed all three of these previous parallel structures into one overarching Nordic defence-cooperation agreement.

NORDEFCO's progress has been slow, but it has started to bear fruit: a Joint Tactical Air Transport Wing is currently planned, having received approval in November 2012.[22] Annual

NORDEFCO–Baltic meetings were established in 2012, following invitations to the Baltic nations to join the grouping in 2011.[23] Various areas for further cooperation have also been outlined, including the development of a joint and combined information infrastructure by 2020, a study on a Nordic Battalion Task Force currently under way, and a plan to find efficiencies in such areas as mine countermeasures, unmanned aerial systems and logistics.

Nordic cooperation in operations is also increasing elsewhere. Finland and Sweden will join Norway and Denmark in the rotational NATO air policing of Iceland from 2014. Three of the Nordic nations (excluding Denmark and Iceland) are members of the EU's Nordic Battlegroup, alongside Estonia and Ireland (Norway is a member of the group, despite not being in the EU). The battlegroup headquarters were inaugurated in 2006, with the group operational in 2008 and 2011 thus far. The peculiarity of a non-EU nation participating in a battlegroup was replicated in Libya in 2011, when non-NATO Sweden joined Denmark and Norway in supporting *Operation Unified Protector*.

The Nordic nations are, by and large, seeing shrinking defence budgets and personnel numbers, which is being countered by the purchase of fewer numbers of high-tech equipment and greater regional defence coordination. There is a greater focus on the Arctic as a potential area of operations, particularly within Norway, but this has yet to translate into a major shift in defence posture.

North America's Arctic presence

Across the Atlantic, Canada has been one of the more vocal Arctic states when discussing issues of sovereignty. In an unusually bellicose statement, in 2007 Canadian Prime Minister Stephen Harper asserted that 'Canada has a choice when it comes to defending our sovereignty in the Arctic. We either use it or lose it. And make no mistake this government intends to use it.'[24]

In parallel with this rhetoric, Ottawa has embarked on Arctic-specific defence-procurement programmes. By far the most significant Canadian military development has been the plan to procure between six and eight ice-strengthened Arctic offshore patrol ships, with the first to be launched in 2015 at a current cost of US$3.1bn. These vessels will not boast substantial offensive-weapons systems; instead, they will be humbly armed offshore patrol vessels intended to bolster Ottawa's ability to secure its territorial sovereignty. Canada is also expected to be a major customer for the F-35 multi-role aircraft programme, with Ottawa planning to buy up to 65 of these aircraft.

At the same time, the Canadian military has attempted to build a more regular presence in the Arctic. A 500-strong army response unit for the Arctic is likely to be formed, and the military expects to construct both a seasonally available deepwater docking/refuelling facility at Nanisivik and an Arctic training centre in Resolute Bay, where the airfield may also be upgraded. The armed forces have also held three recurring exercises in the far north since 2007: *Operations Nanook, Nunalivut* and *Nunakput* are designed to assert Canadian sovereignty, as well as increase Arctic readiness.

Nevertheless, Ottawa's security-force presence in the High North is still relatively modest, comprising the Canadian Rangers, a small army-reserve unit under Joint Task Force North (JTFN), the signals-intelligence facility Canadian Forces Station Alert, and a chain of radars that provides an early-warning system in the north. Part of the expansion of the security-force presence in the High North is to add 300 rangers within JTFN to bring the total to approximately 1,900 (the Rangers as a whole is being expanded by 900 personnel to 5,000, but only a third of these extra troops will be in the north). Moreover, the exercises are merely the reinstatement of a presence that was removed after the Cold War.

The US is even more limited in its Arctic presence and capabilities. There are no bases within the Arctic Circle in the US and no naval bases in Alaska. (The US Army and US Air Force have five locations in Alaska, and the latter uses Thule in Greenland for ballistic-missile defence, which is within the Arctic.) Perhaps the most substantial materiel maintained in Alaska that could be used in a conventional conflict are the F-22 *Raptors* maintained by the USAF's 3rd Wing (90th and 525th Fighter Squadrons) and the 477th Fighter Group (302nd Fighter Squadron) of the Air Force Reserve Command, all based out of Joint Base Elmendorf-Richardson. US Navy surface vessels can operate in northern climes, but none are ice-strengthened.

This paucity of permanently deployed assets is recognised by the Department of Defense (DoD) but no plans are in place to rectify it. According to its Arctic strategy, published in November 2013, the Pentagon will enhance its Arctic operations, in the near term, by 'continuing to conduct exercises and training in the region'. Only in the mid-to-far term is the possibility of 'developing further capabilities and capacity to protect US air, land and maritime borders' even vaguely noted.[25]

The US ballistic-missile and nuclear-powered submarine fleet regularly operated in the Arctic during the Cold War, with USS *Nautilus* being the first vessel to traverse the North Pole and USS *Skate* being the first to surface at the pole, both in 1958. These submarine deployments continue today, and infrequent exercises continue to ensure an irregular presence in the High North. Indeed, it is in the fields of ballistic-missile defence and early warning that the US likely sees the most value in the Arctic. The possibility of sea-based ballistic-missile-defence systems being deployed in the Arctic (particularly around Greenland or Svalbard) is a specific concern for Russia, which fears that it would complicate its strategic-deterrence posture.[26]

The US presence in the Arctic therefore underlines the region's strategic nature, with early-warning radars at Clear, Alaska and Thule, as well as ballistic-missile-defence interceptors in Fort Greely, Alaska, but also reveals the dearth of assets devoted to the region. Regular US exercises occur in or near Alaska, including the USAF's annual *Red Flag Alaska* and the joint-service, annual *Northern Edge* and *Arctic Edge* exercises, but permanently deployed assets are sparse. Canada is more militarily committed to the Arctic, perhaps owing to the emotional and national pride invested in the region by the population, but even Canada's physical presence is likely to remain limited. While Canada has devoted, and will devote, more resources to the High North, its overall posture will remain modest amid the difficult operating conditions found there.

Zone of cooperation

The overview of military forces deployed within the Arctic and current procurement programmes suggest that the region is more important to some countries' defence postures, particularly those of Russia, Norway and Canada. Indeed, the procurement of new SSBNs, nuclear-powered submarines and missile-laden surface combatants does not suggest a primary concern with maritime safety and security, but rather a desire to project power into and beyond the Arctic Ocean. As Putin stated in February 2013, 'the danger of the militarisation of the Arctic also persists.'[27]

However, this should be heavily caveated by the fact that the low levels of spending and relative lack of urgency over the modest increases in Arctic-related purchases and presence seem to reflect a lack of genuine state-based military competition over the region. The recapitalisation of the Russian Northern Fleet may be a concern to neighbouring states, but it could be argued that it is largely designed to update clearly decrepit equipment rather than to build a more muscular Arctic presence with which to coerce its neighbours. Some nations may be warily watching their neighbours, owing to a history of rivalry, but this has not yet developed into a clear action–reaction dynamic.

It may also result from the difficulties of operating and basing forces in the Arctic. The cold weather is unpleasant for personnel and affects the ability of helicopters and aircraft to operate, given the likelihood of icing. White-outs are possible as snow is blown by the rotor wash of a helicopter, while vessels need to be ice-strengthened if operating in waters with floating ice or ice sheet to prevent damage to the hull. Electronic communications can be affected by magnetic and solar interference in the Arctic, while the 24-hour sunlight in summer and darkness in winter can affect visibility. The very remoteness of the region also offers challenges, as it becomes difficult to support deployed troops, while the lack of infrastructure makes transportation by land extremely challenging during certain times of the year.

The various littoral countries of the Arctic are, however, aware of the necessity of governing the increasingly used space in the north. Russia's Arctic Strategy, for example, emphasises that military presence in the region is largely owing to a need to combat terrorism at sea, smuggling and illegal migration ,and for resource protection.[28] This is reflected to some extent in Russia's newest naval shipbuilding programme, which has deprioritised the more ambitious and less necessary ships, such as the aircraft carrier and cruiser programme, in favour of platforms that will enable Moscow to monitor and govern its waters, such as frigates and corvettes. To a large extent, therefore, the growth in military capabilities is relatively restrained and driven more by the knowledge that the retreat of sea ice in the Arctic will create vast areas of water that will require governance as increased traffic will demand safety measures.

While rhetoric about securing national sovereignty is sometimes used, some of the recent procurement and deployments are perceived not only as symbolic assertions of sovereignty, but also as necessary deployments of security forces to prevent the emergence of a large, ungoverned space. The increased military attention in the High North may therefore, at least in part, be a securitisation of the region rather than a militarisation.

The various militaries of the Arctic have, in fact, been more focused on cooperating and building nascent military–military relations than engaging in competitive procurement or gunboat diplomacy. Formal Arctic military cooperation in the post-Cold War era dates back to 1996, when the US, Russia and Norway signed an agreement on Arctic military environmental cooperation, which sought to prevent environmental harm to the region through military (and, in particular, nuclear) activities. Since 2010, Norway has held joint exercises with Russia, through the bilateral *Pomor* series, reflecting Oslo's desire to build a more collaborative military–military relationship with Moscow even as it purchases high-end platforms and weapons. Exercise *Northern Eagle* has been an annual bilateral Russia–US exercise since 2004, but in 2008 it was expanded to include Norway. The second chiefs-of-defence meeting was held in Greenland in June 2013, bringing together the heads of the militaries or coastguards of all eight Arctic nations. The meeting was preceded by a message from Danish Chief of Defence General Peter Bartram, chair of the gathering, who noted that 'we do not want to militarise the Arctic. Quite the opposite.'[29] The meeting led to an agreement to expand maritime surveillance cooperation and joint military exercises. The US-sponsored, annual Arctic Security Forces roundtables also act as a form of confidence building in a region with little security architecture, a fact noted by the US DoD Arctic strategy, which focused heavily on international cooperation and burden sharing to enable objectives to be met with little cost or possibility of deterioration in relations.

Putin himself, often seen as a belligerent voice of Russian nationalism, has highlighted the importance of cooperation in the Arctic and the fact that the region should not be seen as one of competition. Speaking in 2010, Putin suggested that the Arctic should be a 'zone of peace and cooperation', and that 'all the problems existing in the Arctic … can be resolved through an atmosphere of partnership'.[30]

Given the potential riches to be gained from the opening of the Arctic, Moscow is indeed eager to ensure a stable High North that would allow for the continuous and safe economic exploitation of the Arctic. As Yevgeny Lukyanov, a deputy secretary of the Russian Security Council, noted in January 2013, 'Russia needs to cooperate with other Arctic states in strengthening and defending its Arctic borders and in monitoring transportation routes.'[31] As such, Russia has been encouraged to seek collaborative solutions to problems in the region, such as the 2010 Barents Sea agreement between Russia and Norway that was the result of 40 years of negotiation over maritime delimitation of potentially hydrocarbon-rich waters. Russia's desire to utilise the Arctic for commercial purposes means that Moscow is more likely to perceive collaboration as in its interests. The monitoring of traffic through different EEZs along the NEP, for example, would necessitate coordination among constabulary agencies and information sharing.

The fact that NATO has strenuously avoided competition with Russia in the Arctic also reflects this dynamic (as well as the desire of NATO members such as Canada to avoid internationalisation of the region). Although Oslo has encouraged a greater NATO presence there through the *Cold Response* invitational exercises it has hosted since 2006, the organisation has explicitly stated that it will not maintain a permanent presence in the High North. After announcing that NATO would not have a direct presence in the Arctic in May 2013, Secretary-General Anders Fogh Rasmussen noted that 'the Arctic is a hard environment. It rewards cooperation, not confrontation, and I trust we will continue to see cooperation.'[32]

Lack of a security architecture

The current narrative of military–military cooperation and collaboration is not necessarily permanent. The Arctic has been used previously as a theatre for military operations and it is conceivable that it could be used in this way again. Scenarios that might lead to such an outcome usually revolve around a deterioration in the relationship between Russia and other Arctic states or NATO, perhaps owing to regime change in Moscow or the rise of a virulent Russian nationalism. Still, it is currently difficult to conceive of NATO allies, EU member states or close Nordic countries sliding into conflict over the region. This is reflected in the low, but still extant, level of military competition in the region, with Norwegian defence procurement and relations with NATO in particular suggesting a hedging strategy against any possible Russian resurgence in the Arctic.

As such, while the cooperative dynamic currently in play should be welcomed, it should not be taken for granted. The Arctic is an area with the unique potential to foster collaborative relations between the often antagonistic partners of Russia and NATO, but it lacks any form of security architecture in which to embed positive trends. The inability of the Arctic Council to discuss military and security issues under its restricted mandate means that the primary regional forum has opted not to create such an architecture. The chiefs-of-defence meeting and Arctic Security Forces Roundtable could be seen as a nascent attempt to build an architecture, but it is currently piecemeal and Russian attendance at the roundtable is not guaranteed.

The development of such an architecture is innately difficult, given the history of rivalry in the region that could engender mistrust around military issues. Nonetheless, it could be an effective policy to ensure the peaceful development of the region. The creation of regular, ministerial-level meetings, joint exercises and forums through which parties could coordinate activities and share information would be of significant benefit to regional stability. It would serve to reassure the various Arctic states as the inevitable shift of military resources to the region gathers pace in the medium term in order to ensure sovereignty and govern newly active space.

Whether the sensitivities of the Arctic littoral states to cooperation with the three non-littoral states, or mutual mistrust
between Russia and the other states, will prevent such an
architecture from being formed is the main unknown in Arctic
security. For the time being, however, while there remains
suspicion among some Arctic states – and occasional bouts of
belligerent rhetoric and the procurement of some equipment,
which suggests state-based rivalry – the reality is that the Arctic
is not witnessing an uncontrolled or substantially competitive
militarisation. It is a region that has inherent strategic value,
given the patrols of ballistic-missile submarines, but it is also
one in which operations are hampered by weather and geography. While Russian defence spending has increased rapidly, it is
from a remarkably low base and investments are currently just
rejuvenating an entirely dilapidated fleet. Most Nordic budgets
are constrained by austerity, US defence priorities lie elsewhere
and Canada's primary Arctic-focused procurement is of vessels
devoted to maritime security. There may be more military activity in the Arctic in the future, but it is currently far from being a
battleground for rival states.

Notes

1 Richard Vaughan, *The Arctic: A History* (Stroud: Alan Sutton, 2007), p. 203.

2 US Congressional Record, vol. 154, part 18, p. 24292.

3 Basil H. Liddell Hart, *History of the Second World War*, vol. 1 (London: Cassell, 1970), pp. 51–9.

4 Richard Rhodes, *Dark Sun* (New York: Simon and Schuster, 2005), pp. 94–102.

5 Tobias R. Philbin, *The Lure of Neptune: German–Soviet Naval Collaboration and Ambitions, 1919–1941* (Columbia, SC: University of South Carolina Press, 1994), pp. 131–7.

6 *Ibid.*, pp. 132–42.

7 See Carl Bildt, 'Sweden and the Soviet submarines', *Survival*, vol. 25, no. 4, July–August 1983, pp. 165–9, for an overview of these incidents.

8 'Towards a Wider High North: Strategic Issues in a Changing Arctic', in *Strategic Survey 2008: The Annual Review of World Affairs* (Abingdon: Routledge for the IISS, 2008), pp. 58–71; George Lindsey, *Strategic Stability in the Arctic*, Adelphi Paper 241 (London:

Brassey's for the IISS, 1989); David Miller, *The Cold War: A Military History* (London: Pimlico, 2001), pp. 174–80.

9   *The Military Balance 1992–93* (Oxford: Oxford University Press for IISS, 1993); *The Military Balance 2002–03* (Oxford: Oxford University Press for IISS, 2003).

10 Hans M. Kristensen, 'Russian SSBN Fleet: Modernizing But Not Sailing Much', Federation of American Scientists, 3 May 2013, http://blogs.fas.org/security/2013/05/russianssbns/.

11 *The Military Balance 2001–02* (Oxford: Oxford University Press for IISS, 2002) and *The Military Balance 2013* (London: Routledge for IISS, 013).

12 '$4bn hole revealed in Russia's defense spending', *Russia Today*, 7 February 2013.

13 *The Military Balance 2013*, pp. 231–4.

14 Märta Carlsson and Niklas Granholm, 'Russia and the Arctic: Analysis and Discussion of Russian Strategies', Swedish Defence Research Agency, March 2013, pp. 26–8.

15 Alissa de Carbonnel, 'Putin: Russia to reopen Soviet-era Arctic military base', Reuters, 16 September 2013.

16 Katarzyna Zysk, 'Military Aspects of Russia's Arctic Policy: Hard Power and Natural Resources', in James Kraska (ed.), *Arctic Security in an Age of Climate Change* (New York: Cambridge University Press, 2011), pp. 86–7.

17 'Ryskt flyg övade anfall mot Sverige', *Svenska Dagbladet*, 22 April 2013.

18 'Russia sends warships to the Arctic for the first time since Soviet Union break-up', *Daily Mail*, 15 July 2008.

19 *The Military Balance 1992–93* and *The Military Balance 2013*.

20 Gerard O'Dwyer, 'Norway bucks trend as neighbors curb spending', *Defense News*, 24 October 2012.

21 Norwegian Ministry of Defence, 'Norwegian Defence 2008' , p. 7.

22 O'Dwyer, 'Proposed Nordic Joint Tactical Air Transport Wing Progresses', *Defense News*, 23 June 2013.

23 'Baltics invited to join NORDEFCO', *The Baltic Times*, 24 January 2011.

24 'Canada to strengthen Arctic claim', BBC News, 10 August 2007.

25 US Department of Defense, 'Arctic Strategy', November 2013, pp. 7–8.

26 For a detailed discussion on the positioning of ballistic-missile defence in Europe (including the High North), see Dean A. Wilkening, 'Does Missile Defence in Europe Threaten Russia?', *Survival*, vol. 54, no. 1, February–March 2012, pp. 31–52.

27 'Putin sees strategic balance threatened', *United Press International*, 27 February 2013.

28 Zysk, 'Russia's Arctic strategy: ambitions and constraints', *Joint Force Quarterly*, no. 57, 2nd quarter 2010, pp. 103–10.

29 O'Dwyer, 'Greenland meeting highlights Arctic's growing importance', *Defense News*, 2 June 2013.

30 James Brooke, 'Putin Stresses Cooperation in Arctic Resources Disputes', *Voice of America*, 22 September 2010.

31 'Russia calls for Tougher Arctic Security', *RIA Novosti*, 21 January 2013.

32 Mia Bennett, 'Why NATO isn't establishing an Arctic presence', *Alaska Dispatch*, 6 June 2013.

CHAPTER FOUR

Paramilitary and constabulary activity

The mild military transformation of the Arctic, while perhaps not akin to a 'militarisation' that suggests state-based rivalry and procurement competition, does reflect concerns over the possibility of a large, ungoverned space in the north. The lack of large population centres, vast areas of land and sea, increasing human and economic activity and harsh weather conditions make it a difficult region to govern effectively, with safety and security challenging to deliver for both permanent residents and temporary visitors.

The fact that the two agreements reached under the Arctic Council thus far have focused on issues of maritime safety and security, traditionally the purview of constabulary forces, underlines the role that such forces could play in the Arctic. In order to avoid the possibility of a costly and dangerous shift of military resources to the north, it would be sensible for constabulary forces to assume some of the burden for security provision to enable greater economic activity.

However, there have been only limited attempts, varying among the states in their intensity, to encourage greater roles for constabulary forces. There is currently a discrepancy between those states that are prioritising or beginning to prioritise constabulary forces, such as Iceland and the United States, and those that see the issue of the Arctic in more emotional terms and therefore where the military has been the predominant security service, such as Canada and Russia. (In Iceland, law-enforcement activity is the only manner in which security can be delivered, given the lack of a standing military.)

Some multilateral coordination has occurred among these services, but none of it has been Arctic-specific. The question remains whether these law-enforcement agencies will expand in their operations, presence and activity in the High North in order to fill the potential security vacuum that could be created by retreating sea ice. If not, then it is probable that the various militaries might instead fill that role, despite not being the agencies best suited to cope with the intricacies of maritime safety.

The US Coast Guard in the Arctic

It is unsurprising that those countries for which military presence in the Arctic is a lower priority have a stronger emphasis on paramilitary and constabulary agencies in the High North. Given the maritime nature of the region, the non-military agencies that are likely to assume the most significant roles are its various coastguards.

The United States Coast Guard (USCG) is the only constabulary agency that has seen fit to develop a strategy towards the Arctic, which it released in May 2013. Indeed, it is notable that the US Department of Defense released its Arctic strategy six months after the USCG's own strategy, underlining the low priority afforded to this theatre and the fact that the lead role is being played by the coastguard rather than the military. The country with the most well-defined coastguard policy towards the Arctic is therefore also the strongest military power in the world. This may be owing to the large number of commitments the US military has around the world, leaving little room for prioritisation of the Arctic. The US Navy's pivot to Asia underlines the burdens that the military faces in other parts of the world, and the lack of resources and assets for a similar shift to the High North. For other countries, the Arctic assumes a far greater share of their defence burden, given their larger geographical exposure to the region and a dearth of other roles and ongoing military operations.

The USCG has been active in the Arctic since the purchase of Alaska in 1867, with periodic displays of bravado in the region's harsh climate. The overland expedition of 1897 has gone down in the service's history, in which the Revenue Cutter USS *Bear* sailed north and landed a party to rescue 265 trapped whalers.

It should be noted that the USCG is in fact a military service, so its leading role in dealing with the Arctic does not indicate an entire 'demilitarisation' of the issue for the US. Indeed, the USCG is more powerful than many navies: the fact that a decommissioned and aged USCG cutter that was donated in 2012 became the Philippine Navy's flagship hints at the capabilities maintained by the USCG.

Yet in the Arctic there are a number of capability gaps. The USCG 17th District encompasses Alaska, but it operates only one heavy icebreaker (USCGC *Polar Star*), one medium icebreaker (USCGC *Healy*), and only one cutter (USCGC *Alex Haley*) capable of operating in light ice conditions. There is a fleet of ocean-going buoy tenders that are capable of operating in light ice, but no patrol vessels. The USCG maintains Air Station Kodiak and Air Station Sitka, with HC-130H *Hercules* SAR aircraft, MH-60T *Jayhawk* utility helicopters and MH-65D *Dolphin* SAR helicopters.

This lack of ice-capable equipment, particularly in the maritime domain, is exacerbated by a paucity of onshore support infrastructure in light of vast distances that often need to be covered. As the USCG strategy notes:

> Dutch Harbour in the Aleutian Islands is the closest
> US deepwater port to the Arctic; roughly 1,100 nauti-

cal miles from Barrow [the northernmost city in Alaska, and therefore the US]. The closest Coast Guard Air Station to Barrow is located approximately 945 nautical miles south in Kodiak, Alaska.[1]

Across these distances, it takes about four hours for a fixed-wing aircraft or ten hours for a rotary-wing aircraft to reach Barrow, while it takes three days for a USCG cutter to reach the Bering Strait.[2]

There is also little commercial infrastructure that could be used in an emergency. Nome, on the west coast of Alaska (just south of the Arctic Circle), has a small harbour that can host vessels with a draught of just six metres, on a 50-metre pier. This is insufficient in depth to service the USCG's long-endurance cutters (such as the *Hamilton* and *Legend* classes) and insufficient in length to service the medium-endurance cutters (such as the *Famous* and *Reliance* classes), although the length restrictions should be less of a problem than the depth. A pier and loading facility north of the Bering Strait, usually used to support mining operations, can be used, but larger vessels have to anchor offshore; resupply of a USCG cutter, therefore, would likely involve vertical replenishment through the use of a helicopter while the vessel remained at anchor some 12nm offshore. Commercial airports in Nome, Barrow and Prudhoe Bay can act as resupply and refuelling stations for USCG equipment, but not as bases. Only very limited attempts have been made to remedy the situation: in July 2013, it was announced that the USCG would be opening a forward-operating location north of the Bering Strait in Kotzebue, in northwestern Alaska. However, the location will only be available seasonally and will consist only of one MH-60 *Jayhawk* helicopter flying out of the Alaska Air National Guard Hangar in the city.[3]

Given these capability gaps and infrastructural weaknesses, the USCG strategy is explicit in laying out the service's limited objectives in the region over the coming decade: to improve awareness, modernise governance and broaden partnerships. These objectives hint at the difficulties that any one service, even one of the most powerful coastguards in the world, has when operating in the Arctic; the goals of improving awareness and broadening partnerships, which highlight both international cooperation and collaboration with indigenous groups, are essentially burden sharing to ensure a greater provision of security without a significant investment in facilities or equipment.

The USCG strategy, therefore, highlights the need for a greater constabulary presence and focus in and on the Arctic, while also underlining the insufficient capabilities currently in place to accomplish this goal.

Canada's capabilities

Canada also maintains a sizeable coastguard, as the nation with the world's longest coastline. It is, however, a relatively modern service, having been formed only in 1962 (its antecedents run further back, to confederation in 1867). The Canadian Coast Guard (CCG) maintains greater capabilities for operating in ice than the Royal Canadian Navy, which makes the former's focus on procurement of military hardware somewhat bewildering.

The CCG has a fleet of 15 icebreakers, which are regularly called on for duty in ice-covered waters; they escort an average of four vessels per day through ice.[4] These icebreakers are ageing, but a replacement *Polar*-class icebreaker, to be named *John G Diefenbaker*, is scheduled to be ready in 2017, at a cost of US$720 million. The CCG is often the lead for Arctic presence – particularly in the June–November period, when seven icebreakers are deployed to the north – and has the only waterborne environmental-response capacity, placing it in an excellent position to take the lead in the Arctic Council's marine oil-spill response agreement.

Despite these ice-water capabilities, the CCG actually has very little permanent presence in the Arctic. Its northernmost base is in Iqaluit, Nunavut, still south of the Arctic Circle, through which all Arctic maritime communications are maintained. The paucity of Arctic assets led the Standing Senate Committee on Fisheries and Oceans to conclude in 2009 that while 'the main platform for Canadian operations in the Arctic should be CCG ships armed as necessary', it was also true that 'major gaps remain.' According to the Senate report, 'Canada's presence in the Arctic needs to be enhanced in terms of ships, personnel, administration offices, surveillance, shipping regulations, search and rescue (SAR) and oil-spill remediation'.[5] The report particularly highlighted the lack of surveillance aircraft, comprehensive reporting requirements (while acknowledging that the NORDREG vessel-traffic system would be made compulsory in 2010, it still omits smaller vessels under 300-tonnes displacement), and ice-capable patrol vessels for year-round operations.

These capability gaps are recognised and some investment is being directed towards addressing them. The 2012 Economic Action Plan outlined CAD5.2 billion to be spent over the following 11 years to renew the CCG fleet, with purchases including new vessels, helicopters and modernisations. In June 2013, Minister of National Defence Peter McKay announced CAD488m to purchase up to 21 new CCG vessels – all support, auxiliary or SAR craft.

There is a peculiar situation in which the CCG remains the agency most directly responsible for many roles relevant to the Arctic, such as maritime SAR, environmental-disaster response and maritime-traffic control and monitoring. Yet the service's icebreaking fleet is slowly ageing, it lacks ice-capable patrol vessels and the highest-profile Arctic-specific procurement project, the Arctic Offshore Patrol Ships, is being directed toward the Royal Canadian Navy. Nonetheless, it is clear that the CCG will continue to have a leading role in Canadian activity in the High North.

Norway, Iceland and Denmark

The Scandinavian countries with Arctic coastline vary in the extent to which they focus on their law-enforcement agencies as Arctic actors.

For Iceland, there is no other force that can take the lead; the country lacks a standing military and its coastguard is the only security service available for Arctic deployments. The maritime domain has traditionally been very important for Iceland, with an economy heavily dependent on its fishery industry, the second-largest in Europe. The 'cod wars' that were fought intermittently with the United Kingdom from the 1950s until the 1970s demonstrated the utility of Iceland's coastguard. The Icelandic Coast Guard (ICG) is a small force, with just four vessels and one fixed-wing aircraft, so despite the fact that Iceland is entirely within the Arctic under the AHDR definition, it has only a limited constabulary presence in the region. Although Iceland remains outside the maximum sea-ice-extent area, both the two *Aegir*-class patrol vessels and the ICG's new flagship, *Thor*, delivered in 2011, are ice-strengthened, enabling them to be deployed to the east coast of Greenland in light ice.

By contrast, and perhaps unusually for a country that boasts one of the world's largest shipping companies – in Maersk, Denmark – does not have a coastguard, and the various maritime constabulary roles are spread across a number of agencies. The Danish Maritime Authority, for example, is in charge of pollution prevention and the administration of maritime traffic in Danish waters. While the 2008 self-government referendum in Greenland devolved coastguard duties to Nuuk, there are no maritime assets maintained by the Greenlandic government to uphold these responsibilities. (Air Greenland maintains just two SAR helicopters – one S-61 in Kangerlussuaq and one Bell 212 in South Greenland.) This, in essence, creates a vast maritime space in which there is little environmental-response or SAR capability. (Greenland has attempted to rectify this situation somewhat through the purchase of two EC225 helicopters as replacements that will allow the government to more effectively fulfil its obligations under the 2011 SAR agreement.)

Significant questions remain about the ability of either Denmark or Greenland to handle an oil spill. A Danish Ministry of Defence report leaked in December 2012 underlined concerns over the viability of the two ageing environmental-response vessels, the *Gunnar Seidenfaden* and the *Gunnar Thorson*, both of which are due to be decommissioned in 2015. When MV *Fu Shan Hai* sank off the Danish island of Bornholm in 2003, the Swedish maritime authorities were the lead agency in the oil-spill response.[6] An assessment of the ability of Denmark and Greenland to respond to an oil spill off the Greenlandic coast suggests that just 5,000 tonnes of oil per day could be handled.[7]

Denmark therefore has significant capability gaps in the roles normally ascribed to a coastguard. Norway, however, has a coastguard under the auspices of the navy that boasts a number of different patrol vessels. The KV *Svalbard* is in fact the largest vessel in the Norwegian armed forces and is capable of icebreaking. Beyond the *Svalbard*, another 13 offshore patrol vessels are available, all with armaments of varying levels. Oslo is also significantly upgrading its SAR capabilities, with a decision for procurement of a new long-range, all-weather helicopter to be made by the end of 2013, with the first new aircraft delivered by 2016 and the current *Sea Kings* phased out by 2020. Two *Super Pumas* for SAR will be based on Svalbard from 2014. The Norwegian coastguard is therefore a capable force tasked with fisheries-protection, SAR, environmental-response, customs and sovereignty missions. This to some extent clarifies the reasons for the military procurement that Norway has recently undertaken, which does not appear to be for constabulary roles. However, it also hints at the Norwegian government's investment in, and willingness to undertake, constabulary roles in the High North.

Russia's non-military agencies

For Russia, the situation is slightly more complex. The coast-guard in Russia is within the Federal Border Guard, itself part of the Federal Security Services (FSB), a well-equipped paramilitary force. Its maritime force boasts a fleet of frigates, corvettes and missile and torpedo craft, making it one of the most heavily armed coastguards in the world. While this quasi-military force is spread across Russia's vast coastline, its Arctic presence is gradually being bolstered. It was announced in 2012 that another 20 Arctic border posts would be created in order to assist with maritime surveillance and SAR.[8] This number appeared to have been reduced by mid-2013, when the FSB claimed that 11 border-protection facilities would be created in the Arctic, but also that four new Arctic-specific vessels would be built for the coast guard by 2020.[9]

The Federal Border Guard has the primary responsibility for border control, resource protection and security. Indeed, it was the FSB that arrested 30 people – two journalists and 28 activists – on board the Greenpeace ship *Arctic Sunrise* as they approached and attempted to scale the Gazprom-owned Prirazlomnaya oil platform, in the Pechora Sea, in September 2013.[10] The arrest was a high-profile demonstration of Moscow's unwillingness to allow disruption of its economic exploitation of the Arctic.

Other roles, such as environmental response and SAR, are shared by separate governmental agencies, particularly the Federal Air Transport Agency and the Federal Agency for Marine and River Transport. Furthermore, Russia's nuclear-icebreaker fleet is operated by Atomflot, a federal enterprise. The ability to conduct SAR operations for a stranded cruise ship, for instance, might be spread across a number of agencies within Russia, complicating the bureaucratic picture.

Nevertheless, it is clear that Russia has a sizeable paramilitary force for use in the Arctic and a number of assets that might be called upon for constabulary duties in the High North. There is, however, little onshore infrastructure to maintain permanently deployed personnel and equipment across the NSR, which makes it more difficult to provide comprehensive maritime-traffic monitoring, surveillance and protection.

The Arctic Council agreements

The variety of capabilities available to the various law-enforcement and paramilitary agencies highlights the differing levels of importance Arctic actors place on these services.

These agencies have been prioritised in the only two agreements negotiated under the Arctic Council's auspices, which have been designed to encourage cross-border cooperation on maritime safety and security issues. Both the 2011 SAR agreement and 2013 marine oil-pollution preparedness and response agreement require closer collaboration among the littoral states to ensure the most effective response to any accident or emergency that might occur. The fact that these two topics were the foci of the first binding agreements under the aegis of the council was intriguing, given that the organisation explicitly excludes discussion of security and defence issues from its mandate, largely to avoid the potentially contentious issue of Arctic military deployments. Thus, the conclusion of these agreements suggests that the Council is eager to encourage greater activity by law-enforcement agencies in the Arctic.

The agreements themselves encourage signatories to take a variety of actions. The 2011 SAR agreement mandates the sharing of information and experience that may be beneficial in SAR operations, encourages regular meetings among the parties to build interoperability and lays out the process for requests to cross another state's border in SAR missions. The agreement also delineates the responsibilities for SAR missions of the various parties involved. The 2013 oil marine pollution preparedness-and-response agreement mandates signatories to maintain a minimum level of oil-spill response equipment, monitor for potential spills, facilitate transit through territory, share information and assist other states when requested.

In drawing up the agreements, state parties listed their competent authorities and relevant agencies to respond to such events. For the 2013 agreement, these agencies are largely either the maritime constabulary agencies or relevant civilian departments, such as those of the interior, fisheries or the environment (the exception being Denmark, where the defence ministry is the designated competent authority for spills outside three nm from its coastline). For the 2011 agreement, the competent authorities are all civilian agencies, aside from that of Canada, where the Department of National Defence is the authority. The designated SAR agencies include a number of coastguards (from Canada, Finland, Iceland and the US) and just two military forces (from Canada and the US). Norway's designated SAR agency is the Joint Rescue Coordination Centre, Northern Norway, which is administered by the Ministry of Justice and Public Security, not the military or the coastguard; Russia has designated the Federal Air Transport Agency and the Federal Agency for Marine and River Transport.

The inclusion of so many constabulary and non-military agencies hints at the role that law-enforcement forces can play in the Arctic, and also the recognition among Arctic states that prioritisation of the military may be an unnecessary provocation in the region. It is notable that Russia designates its Federal Air Transport Agency and Federal Agency for Marine and River Transport as the primary SAR agencies, thereby more clearly delineating the boundary- and sovereignty-protection roles of the armed forces and the well-armed Border Guards, and the constabulary roles of these civilian organisations.

Indeed, non-military or paramilitary agencies can be useful tools in confidence building among countries that may otherwise harbour mistrust of one another. They encourage cross-border communication on issues that are of shared interest

– usually focused on maritime security, resource protection and conservation or environmental issues – and therefore appear uncontroversial. It is also easier to coordinate activities using constabulary or environmental agencies rather than militaries, which jealously guard secrets and view each other with unease.

There are therefore ancillary benefits to the 2011 and 2013 agreements beyond making the Arctic theoretically a more secure and safe place for shipping and wildlife. Information sharing, in particular, and the fact that the marine oil-spill agreement includes obligations, for the first time, on minimum capability to be maintained, reassures neighbouring countries that the burden of responsibility may be shared and that they will not be negatively affected by another state's negligence.

There are potential disadvantages to a focus on coastguards or law-enforcement agencies; it is feasible that collaboration will remain stuck at one particular level, never progressing to closer military–military cooperation. In the Arctic, this is less of a concern as military–military ties are already developing, as outlined in Chapter Three. Nonetheless, the effect of closer non-military cooperation could be satisfying the political demand for collaboration while stymying further cross-border relationship building.

The Arctic Council agreements do appear to be tentative steps towards closer regional constabulary collaboration. They seem to suggest a realisation that law-enforcement organisations can be agents for collaboration and confidence building. The council's first two agreements specifically focused on constabulary issues, where they could have rather centred on issues of pollution monitoring, joint scientific expeditions or a host of other, less paramilitary issues.

Multilateral coordination

Whether this collaboration will continue is as yet unclear. No constabulary organisation has been formed, nor has there been any regular law-enforcement engagement specific to the Arctic.

Outside of the two agreements, therefore, there has been a decided lack of specific cross-border collaboration among the various constabulary agencies. There is no specific Arctic coast-guard or constabulary-agency forum. Two related forums exist, namely the North Pacific Coast Guard Forum (NPCGF) and the North Atlantic Coast Guard Forum (NACGF), which include all of the Arctic states among their members. However, the NPCGF excludes the European states and includes Japan, China and South Korea; the NACGF includes all eight Arctic Council members, but also a further 12 European states, which complicates and dilutes the Arctic focus.

It is feasible that the two Arctic Council agreements will begin to forge a nascent constabulary collaboration. There has even been tentative discussion among a handful of commentators of the creation of an Arctic Coast Guard Forum.[11] This remains a somewhat distant goal; the NPCGF and the NACGF have proven to be relatively successful organisations, with mandates that extend to illegal trafficking, piracy, fishery protection, migration and a range of other maritime-security issues. The two Arctic Council agreements, while positive first steps towards developing Arctic-specific cooperation on roles that often sit within the auspices of coastguards, are far from the extensive list of topics dealt with by, and therefore necessitating, the forums in the North Pacific and the North Atlantic.

Furthermore, the fact that some countries (such as Denmark) lack coastguards or the broad range of agencies that partake in the missions and roles often ascribed to coastguards, such as Russia's various civilian agencies, makes it difficult, if not impossible, to create a regional coastguard cooperation mechanism.

It is possible to conceive of closer cooperation among those maritime agencies that do exist. There has been some very sporadic collaboration between coastguard vessels and military forces already. In the *Pomor* 2013 exercises, for example, the Norwegian coastguard vessel KV *Senja* took part alongside a Norwegian frigate, a Russian destroyer and Russian naval infantry.[12] Similarly, in *Pomor* 2011, the Norwegian coastguard vessel KV *Andenes* played an important role, acting as the ship that was boarded by Russian and Norwegian troops.[13] Such interactions are irregular, however, and, given the position of the Norwegian coastguard as a branch of the navy, do not indicate constabulary-specific exercises.

Separately, the US and Canadian coastguards have a close relationship. Joint exercises occur regularly and joint operations happen, on occasion, when it is necessary to utilise assets under the auspices of both organisations for missions such as SAR. The two coastguards are also the custodian agencies of the Canada–United States Joint Marine Pollution Contingency Plan. *Operation Nanook* has sometimes involved Canadian and US coastguard vessels, such as *Nanook* 2010, which saw USCGC *Alder* deployed alongside the CCGS *Henry Larsen*, as well as Danish, Canadian and US military vessels. (Prior to 2010, *Nanook* had been a Canadian Armed Forces and Canadian Coast Guard joint exercise, in which international partners were not invited to participate.) The USCG also works with other Canadian law-enforcement agencies, signing, for example, a cross-border maritime law-enforcement agreement ('Shiprider') with the Royal Canadian Mounted Police in June 2013 that allows for cross-border hot pursuit.

The future of Arctic constabulary forces

The focus on constabulary roles in the first two Arctic Council agreements suggests that there is scope for greater collaboration among the range of forces in the region.

The wide variety of different forces makes it somewhat difficult to envisage a regional forum through which these agencies could collaborate. In particular, the lack of a Danish coastguard means that any regional organisation would necessarily have to be a military–paramilitary forum. Yet Denmark was integral to the creation of the NACGF in 2007 (along with other Nordic nations) and hence it would not be impossible to create an Arctic Coast Guard Forum.

There are other areas where agreements could be reached that would further collaboration over constabulary issues. There is currently no fisheries-conservation or regulation agreement under the auspices of the Arctic Council, and as sea ice retreats in the central Arctic Ocean, this is likely to be seen as more necessary. (All fish within national 200nm EEZs are, of course, already regulated by the coastal state, albeit also subject to trans-boundary conservation and management agreements in many cases.) A small area within the Arctic is, in fact, already regulated by a separate body – the Northeast Atlantic Fisheries Commission – comprising Denmark, Iceland, Norway, Russia and the EU (with Canada, New Zealand and St Kitts and Nevis as cooperating parties). The Arctic Council would be the most likely forum through which to exercise such an agreement, although, given the possibility of other Asian and European countries taking advantage of the catch in the central Arctic Ocean, it would necessarily have to involve them in the discussion. Any agreement could, theoretically, encourage greater constabulary engagement among the Arctic states, at the very least through greater information-sharing and monitoring activity. There have been various statements of support for such an agreement from the Arctic states, but at a meeting of officials from the A5 in Washington in April–May 2013 (bearing in mind that the A5 that will have the greatest say in the matter, as the littoral states will see their interests threatened most by international fishing in the Arctic Ocean), the chairman's statement noted that a further regional fisheries-management organisation was not necessary. Yet it also noted that such an organisation may become necessary in the future, and that interim measures should be put in place that encourage the development of regional or sub-regional fisheries-management organisations.[14]

Other areas for future collaboration could include information sharing on migration, trafficking and smuggling, or, perhaps more appropriately, on piracy and threats to international shipping – an area that Russia would be more eager to engage in, given its desire to open up the NSR.

Such agreements would foster greater cooperation among the various constabulary agencies of the region and help to start differentiating between the role of military forces (namely, border protection and sovereignty missions) and that of non-military or paramilitary forces (including on constabulary, environmental and emergency missions). This need not exclude military forces from those operations where they may be called upon, such as emergency response, given their extensive capabilities, but it would encourage a separation of missions among the various agencies, and would build greater confidence that the primary agency for activity in the High North would be a law-enforcement agency.

This is likely to be an incremental and slow-moving process, however. It will probably occur in lockstep with any military–military relations that are developed. The two trends are not inseparable, but can be seen as mutually reinforcing: as countries become more confident about the intent and presence of their neighbours, they may also feel more confident about embracing areas of collaboration.

Of course, such a process could be derailed if states chose to use the Arctic for more belligerent purposes. Nuclear submarines will still sail the waters of the Arctic Ocean with little diplomatic complaint, but an increased ballistic-missile-defence presence would unnerve Russia and undermine any attempts to engage it militarily and through non-military agencies. The gradual process of collaboration is not irreversible. While the benefits of such a process are relatively evident, it remains to be seen whether the various states will continue to further the process and view constabulary collaboration as a high enough priority in the medium term.

Notes

1   USCG, 'United States Coast Guard Arctic Strategy', May 2013, p. 14, http://www.uscg.mil/seniorleadership/DOCS/CG_Arctic_Strategy.pdf.

2   Paul F. Campagna, Dave McNulty and Heath Roscoe, 'When the Ice Melts', *Proceedings Magazine*, July 2013, p 29.

3   Carey Restino, 'Coast Guard Opens Arctic Operations Center in Kotzebue', *Alaska Dispatch*, 21 July 2013.

4   Canadian Coast Guard website, http://www.ccg-gcc.gc.ca/eng/Central_Arctic/About_Us.

5   'Controlling Canada's Arctic waters: role of the Canadian Coast Guard', report of the Standing Senate Committee on Fisheries and Oceans, December 2009, pp. viii–ix, http://www.parl.gc.ca/content/sen/committee/402/fish/rep/rep07dec09-e.pdf.

6   Christian Wenande, 'Grave concerns over oil spill response capability', *Copenhagen Post*, 17 December 2012.

7   'Arctic oil-spill preparedness called into doubt', *Copenhagen Post*, 25 June 2013.

8   'Russia to set up Arctic frontier posts', *Russia Today*, 16 April 2012.

9   'Russia to deploy 4 new Arctic warships by 2020', *RIA Novosti*, 27 May 2013.

10 Mark Mackinnon, 'Both Canadian Greenpeace activists arrested in Russia now granted bail', *Globe and Mail*, 21 November 2013.

11 Olin Strader and Alison Weisburger, 'Channeling Arctic Indigenous Peoples' Knowledge Into an Arctic Region Security Architecture', Arctic Institute, 13 February 2012, http://www.thearcticinstitute.org/2012/02/channeling-arctic-indigenous-peoples.html.

12 Trude Pettersen, 'Norwegian-Russian POMOR-2013 naval exercise starts this week', *Barents Observer*, 7 May 2013.

13 Trude Pettersen, 'Norwegian-Russian naval exercises successful and effective', *Barents Observer*, 23 May 2011.

14 'Chairman's statement at meeting on future Arctic fisheries', US Department of State, Bureau of Oceans and International Environmental and Scientific Affairs, 1 May 2013, http://www.state.gov/e/oes/rls/pr/2013/209176.htm.

CHAPTER FIVE

Geopolitical impacts of the changing Arctic

The discussion thus far has focused on change: climatic, economic, military and constabulary. At the heart of all this, however, is geographic change, through the seasonal retreat of sea ice, the warming of the seas and shifts in the demography, fauna and flora of the Arctic.

This in turn is changing the politics of the region, both within the Arctic and between it and the rest of the world. The growing strategic significance of the Arctic is encouraging broader interest in the region from below the 66°N-latitude line, while the possibility of economic exploitation is affecting how indigenous populations interact with their nation-states and how Arctic states interact with one another.

The geographic allure of the Arctic is also growing. Climate change in the region has the potential to shift global maritime trade routes, thereby creating new political relationships modelled on new economic opportunities. The fact that Singapore, an equatorial country, saw fit to appoint an Arctic ambassador in January 2012 demonstrates the wide-ranging impact that change in the region may have. Singapore was also among the six nations granted observer status on the Arctic Council in May 2013 – and the only one without a significant history of scientific research on Arctic matters.

National strategies

Nothing illustrates the growing interest in the Arctic better than the fact that all of the Arctic states, as well as the EU, have published new or updated Arctic strategy documents since 2008.[1] These strategies tend to cover many of the same themes, although there are interesting differences among them.[2] The five littoral states stress sovereignty and national security, and for Canada and the United States these are the primary concerns. The non-littoral states and the EU, on the other hand, stress comprehensive security. All nine strategies emphasise economic development, environmental protection and international cooperation, particularly within the Arctic Council. Most stress regional development and infrastructure, governance and management, and peoples or cultures. Finland, Iceland, Russia and the US all prioritise maritime shipping and transportation, while Finland, Iceland, Russia, Denmark and Norway all stress maritime safety. Science and scientific cooperation are explicitly mentioned by Iceland, Norway, the US and Russia (see Table 1.1).

These national policy differences stem from demography, economics, history, culture and politics. The common themes, especially the focus on development and cooperation, augur well for a peaceful regional future, but these are generalities. Only detailed analysis of the economic opportunities – as well as military and paramilitary roles, functions and capabilities in the region – can tell us where on the spectrum between cooperation and confrontation the future of Arctic geopolitics and governance lies.

Table 1.1 **Priority areas identified in Arctic Strategies of the A8**

	Canada	Denmark	Finland	Iceland	Norway	Russia	Sweden	US
Sovereignty and national security	x	x			x	x		x
Comprehensive Security	x	x	x	x	x			x
Economic development	x	x	x	x	x	x	x	x
Regional development and infrastructure	x	x	x	x	x	x	x	
Sea transportation and aviation			x	x		x		x
Environment and environmental protection	x	x	x	x	x		x	x
Governance and management	x	x		x	x	x	x	x
Rescue and safety	x	x		x	x	x		x
Peoples in general			x	x			x	
Indigenous peoples			x	x		x	x	x
Science, technology, knowledge and cooperation				x	x	x		x

Source: Heininen 2011, Table 7, updated to include 2013 US Arctic Strategy.

How this geopolitical change will manifest is not yet clear. The changes in the Arctic are creating tensions, but also areas for assurance, among the Arctic states and with extra-regional countries. Some countries are being empowered and others disempowered by the transformation of the region, while supra-national organisations are attempting to make their presence felt.

Geopolitics of the north

An early proponent of the concept of geopolitics, the British geographer and parliamentarian Halford Mackinder, viewed the north of the Eurasian continent, largely what is now Russia, Central Asia and at times Eastern European states, as a 'heartland' or 'pivot' around which control of Eurasia centred.[3] This area was landlocked, as far as Mackinder was concerned, given the impassability of the Arctic Ocean.

Mackinder's view differed substantially from that of other geostrategists. Alfred Thayer Mahan, for instance, focused on the importance of sea power to a country's position,[4] while Nicholas J. Spykman suggested it was essentially the Rimland (along the Eurasian coast) that provided the source of control for global powers. Spykman infamously noted that geography was 'the most fundamentally conditioning factor because of its relative permanence'.[5]

The theories of geopolitics have attracted wide-ranging criticism that they rely on geographic determinism, represent a realist, zero-sum world view and show a lack of intellectual rigour. Nonetheless, the subject still has adherents in the post-Cold War era. Zbigniew Brzezinski, who served as national security adviser to US President Jimmy Carter, published *The Grand Chessboard* in 1997, in which he laid out similarly defined geographical areas of the Eurasian continent, describing Russia as the 'black hole' because of its inaccessibility (determined, in large part, by its lack of access to the sea).[6] Robert D. Kaplan published a book in 2010 suggesting that the Indian Ocean was now the area of greatest strategic importance to the determination of power.[7]

Whether or not one agrees with the concept of geopolitics as these writers have defined it, it is certainly true that significant changes in geography can affect political constellations and hierarchies. In fact, it is evident that a major change in geography (which is extremely rare) can dramatically improve or worsen a country's access to trade and to other areas of the world. Thus, the geographical changes being wrought upon the Arctic are likely to affect the interactions of the states, communities and interested actors of the region and beyond.

The country that will be most significantly affected is the one which has the most significant Arctic territory: Russia. More than 50% of the Arctic coastline and approximately 60% of the land in the Arctic lies within Russian territory.[8] Russia also has access to four other seas and oceans through its extensive coastline: the Baltic, Caspian and Black seas and the Bering Sea/Sea of Okhotsk/Pacific Ocean, only the latter of which allows Russia access to the open ocean without having to pass through other countries' territorial waters. But a more open Arctic has the opportunity to transform Russia's access to trade and the sea. As Caitlyn Antrim has suggested, 'the Arctic has played an essential, yet unrecognised, role as the northern wall in the Western strategy to enclose and contain the world's largest land power.'[9] Climate change in the Arctic has the potential to, as Antrim puts it, 'breach the fourth wall of containment' and create an open space that cannot be constrained by outside powers, given its extent. At the same time, this creates a new, fourth front that requires defence for a country traditionally worried, sometimes to the point of paranoia, about foreign encirclement and encroachment.

It also, theoretically, removes a geographical barrier that had previously separated the Arctic states, which should encourage greater interaction, for good or ill. It would be as if the Himalayan mountains were suddenly reduced to mere foothills, and the ancient civilisations of China and South Asia could commune to a far greater extent than before. This would rapidly emphasise the various disputes that already existed in the Sino-Indian relationship and make their resolution a much more immediate concern. But it could also develop far closer interaction among the populations and foster trade and understanding between rivals. This is by and large the process we see under way in the Arctic, where great stress has been placed on decades-old disputes in the short term, but the longer-term focus has been on potential benefits gained through cross-border traffic and communication.

As the largest Arctic state, Russia has the potential to use the region for diplomatic gain and influence, alongside and because of the obvious economic benefits. Competition for influence clearly exists in the form of the US and Canada, but these countries either lack an extensive Arctic presence (the former) or the willingness to open up trade routes to develop economic leverage. The Nordic countries, dwarfed by Russia, struggle to compete for international, or even regional, influence.

Russia, by contrast, can use the Arctic both to increase its influence on global shipping lanes and to encourage closer ties with the Nordic countries, thereby gently fracturing the European/ NATO alliances in the north.

One of the problems for Moscow is deciding the best method for achieving these goals: bilateralism or multilateralism. The fact that every country in the Arctic bar Russia can be seen through the prism of Euro-Atlantic 'Western' culture and multilateral institutions, such as the EU and NATO, means it is easy for Moscow to feel isolated in the north and mistrustful of multilateral intervention. In addition, Moscow traditionally would favour bilateral interactions with the Nordic nations to leverage its superior size. This preference for bilateralism is moderated somewhat by shifts in Russia's foreign policy since the end of the Cold War and the peculiarities of the Arctic. Post-Cold War Russia has been more willing to work through potentially restrictive international organisations; it joined the IMF in 1992 and the World Trade Organization in 2012. At the same time, the cross-border effects of climate change and the desire of other Arctic nations to build regional governance and maintain their positions in multilateral alliances has meant Russia has also had to act through international forums such as the Arctic Council or the Barents Euro-Arctic Council. This should be caveated by noting that the Arctic Council remains an intergovernmental forum rather than an international organisation, given the difficulties in coordinating a disparate set of countries with a variety of interests and priorities in the region.

Indeed, the Arctic nations have never been a cohesive group. The Cold War effectively estranged Russia from other Arctic states, and differing perceptions of the level and immediacy of the threat from the Soviet Union between those Nordic states on its border and the North American states meant that there was a lack of coherent policy towards Moscow. Sweden's avowed neutrality, for example, sat uneasily with the more simplistic calculations with regard to the Soviet Union in the US and other NATO states.

In the post-Cold War environment, this situation has been complicated by Russia's inclusion in NATO's Partnership for Peace (PfP) programme in 1994. Equally, the growing defence cooperation among the Nordic states and the eastward expansion of both the EU and NATO since 1991 have done little to assuage Moscow's concerns over a Western-centric system that does not represent Russian interests. Issues such as ballistic-missile defence in Europe only reinforce Moscow's sense that Western states still see relations with Russia in zero-sum terms.

The opening of the Arctic therefore presents an opportunity for Russia to not only capitalise on newly accessible resource and trade wealth, but also to attempt to use its pivotal position in the region to develop a greater influence among a small number of EU and NATO states. It also provides Russia with a more flexible geostrategic position, with greater access to the sea from a larger number of points. The potentially global effects of the NEP could help bolster Russia's profile and influence over a number of extra-regional states, particularly those in Northeast Asia.

NATO and the US

Russia is not the only Arctic state whose political focus vacillates between bilateralism and multilateralism. Norway, in particular, has had a somewhat schizophrenic policy that attempts to balance its bilateral relations with Russia, as exemplified in regular military–military visits, with its involvement in multilateral institutions.

Indeed, Oslo has been at the forefront of encouraging a greater NATO presence in the Arctic by inviting all Alliance members and some PfP members to take part in its *Cold Response* exercises, in order to balance Russia's growing military capabilities. That NATO has been less than eager to agree to a permanent or bolstered presence is due not only to a concern over its relations with Russia (Moscow strongly disagrees with the idea that the world's foremost military alliance should be involved in the north), but also to disagreement among NATO members about the organisation's role in the region.

Canada, for example, has attempted to discourage greater NATO involvement in the region, most likely to avoid a wider discussion of its remaining disputes over Hans Island, the Beaufort Sea and the NWP. In fact, in 2009, as NATO was considering its role in the Arctic following the Russian flag-planting two years earlier, a paragraph on the Arctic had been devised for inclusion in the declaration of the Strasbourg–Kehl summit. But, as Helga Haftendorn notes:

> On the eve of the summit meeting on orders of PM
> Harper, Canadian Ambassador Robert McRae had
> to withdraw his consent and request to drop the
> whole para[graph] on the Arctic. This move came as
> a complete surprise to participants and journalists
> alike who had been briefed to expect a reference to the
> Polar region … With the argument that it exercised
> national sovereignty over its Northern provinces and
> the adjoining waters, Canada from there on strictly
> refused to have the NATO Council deal with any
> Arctic issues.[10]

Other states have mixed feelings about the role of NATO in
the High North. Sweden and Finland, as non-members, view a
NATO role as unnecessary (both, however, have participated
in *Cold Response*) and, even in a distant scenario in which both
countries join NATO, this stance would likely remain in order
to avoid antagonising Russia. Iceland, which relies on a NATO
air-policing measure for its own sovereignty, has little say
about favouring some form of intervention for NATO. For the
US, NATO's presence is closely tied to the broader issue of US–
Russia relations.

It is unclear how the geographic change in the Arctic might
affect US–Russia relations. The proposed 'reset' of the relationship
touted by then-Secretary of State Hillary Clinton and Minister of
Foreign Affairs Sergei Lavrov in 2009 has had some successes,
but failed to meet the lofty rhetoric at its initiation in diminish-
ing mistrust between the two powers. The reset came about after
approximately a decade of steadily worsening relations that had
been punctuated by the mistrust over the US withdrawal from
the Anti-Ballistic Missile Treaty in 2002, the seemingly relentless
expansion of NATO, the cyber attacks on Estonia in 2007, the
Russia–Georgia war of 2008 and, perhaps most significantly, the
US plan to use Poland and the Czech Republic as sites for ballistic-

missile-defence facilities. Underlying much of this mistrust was a perception of a newly assertive Russia, first under President Vladimir Putin and then under his successor, Dmitry Medvedev, and a realpolitik-focused US under President George W. Bush. The reset, initially promising when the New Strategic Arms Reduction Treaty was signed in 2010, has since faltered, with the ongoing issue of ballistic-missile defence being a primary point of contention. The Arctic is an area where the US and Russia can potentially agree on a variety of issues, but equally one where the issue of ballistic-missile defence could easily lead to the further deterioration of relations. Until the trajectory of US–Russia relations is clarified, it is unlikely that Washington will support a stronger NATO presence in the Arctic.

Littoral versus Arctic

A further lack of cohesion among Arctic states is apparent over the issues of geographical proximity to the Arctic Ocean.

The Arctic Council, founded in 1996, is now the unrivalled regional forum for discussion of Arctic issues. However, it was not always apparent that the council would be the primary instrument of governance.

In particular, the distinction between the Arctic littoral states (Arctic five or A5) and the wider Arctic eight has created uncertainty over multilateral forums. The A5, understandably, have felt somewhat protective over the issues related to the Arctic Ocean specifically, given that the majority of sea-based resources currently reside in their EEZs, and it is through these zones and, at times, these countries' territorial waters that the two most feasible transit routes will pass. However, this jealous guardianship of a large section of Arctic issues has created a sense of exclusion among the three other council members.

This reached its zenith in 2008, when the A5 met in Ilulissat, Greenland. The resulting declaration noted that the A5 are 'in a unique position to address these possibilities and challenges' of the Arctic and that UNCLOS is a sufficient legal regime to govern the ocean itself.[11]

The effect of the Ilulissat Declaration was to more firmly cement the theme of peaceful collaboration among the Arctic states and the primacy of international law when dealing with sea-based disputes. The timing of the declaration was important, occurring less than a year after the Russian flag-planting episode on the Arctic seabed. The declaration therefore played an important role in easing tensions in the region generally.

However, it also caused discontent among the non-littoral states. It raised 'uncertainty ... regarding the place and the maintenance of the developed driving force of the Arctic Council', while seeming to suggest that the littoral states had a greater role in the affairs of the Arctic than the three Nordic, non-littoral states.[12] It was noticeable that at the second meeting of A5 foreign ministers in Chelsea, near Montreal, Canada, in 2010, it was specifically noted that the A5 format 'by no means belittles the role of the Arctic Council that also includes Sweden, Finland and Iceland'.[13] (Ironically, the meeting in and of itself seemed to formalise the concept of an A5 grouping, and in turn also galvanised the various Arctic states to strengthen the council in order to placate the non-littoral states, with the 2011 search-and-rescue agreement the most concrete example of broader A8 collaboration.)

The Ilulissat meeting highlighted one further aspect of littoral/non-littoral geopolitics: the position of Greenland. Since the end of the Second World War, Greenland has been inching ever closer to independence, with its acceptance as part of Denmark and loss of colony status in 1953, a 1979 initial referendum on home rule leading to the establishment of a Greenlandic parliament and control over certain policy areas, and a 2008 referendum leading to self-government in all areas, except foreign, defence and security policy; exchange-rate and monetary policy; the constitution; nationality; and the Supreme Court.

There remains, however, a strong movement for full independence in Greenland, which is supported by Copenhagen. The difficulty in the short term is the reliance of Greenland on Danish largesse, with approximately 50% of its budget hailing from Denmark. The development of alternative industries, including mineral and hydrocarbon extraction, and tourism, may help Greenland develop a more sustainable and self-sufficient economy and thus encourage the case for independence in the medium-to-long term. The 2013 election, which saw the pro-mining Siumut Party become the largest in the Greenlandic parliament, should encourage the development of the extractive industry, although reservations about foreign labour may prevent some overseas investment.[14]

The possibility of Greenlandic independence only further complicates the Arctic geopolitical map. Denmark would no longer be an Arctic Ocean littoral state, but would likely retain Arctic status through the Faroe Islands, a self-governing country within Denmark that lies within the AMAP/AHDR Arctic line. There would then be nine members of the Arctic Council and still five Arctic Ocean littoral states, but one of them would no longer be an EU member, nor most likely a NATO member (even though there may still be a US air base on the island at Thule). This could therefore give rise to a complicated geopolitical situation in which a small (in population and economy), often social-democratic state would be alongside the world's largest economy, two of the largest countries in the world and one of the richest European nations as an Arctic littoral state. It would be a severe challenge for Greenland to resist the influence of its larger and more powerful Arctic neighbours in such an instance and this, in turn, could affect how Russia sees itself within the region. The fact that Greenland boycotted the Kiruna meting in 2013 as Sweden refused to give its representatives equal weighting with the Arctic states is an indication that, even without independence, Nuuk may seek a seat at the Arctic table.

At present, such a situation remains hypothetical, but very feasible. As such, there are likely to be further changes to the Arctic geopolitical landscape in the years to come.

The role of China

Greenland's circumstances raise further interesting points about Arctic geopolitics, namely the role and influence of extra-regional powers.

One of the issues raised in the 2013 Greenlandic election campaign was the possibility of an influx of migrant labour, particularly Chinese labour, to assist in resource exploitation. The winning Siumut Party campaigned against legislation passed in December 2012 that would allow the large-scale immigration of workers in the mining sector.[15]

Such issues highlight one of the major trends in regional geopolitics: the involvement of China. Chinese companies have been active in Greenland, with Jiangxi Copper, China's largest copper producer, a partner in exploration with the United Kingdom's Nordic Mining Corporation for base metals at Wegner Halvø, on the east coast. (Jiangxi Copper has formed a company with Jiangxi Zhongrun Mining, which supplied the original funding for Nordic in 2009, named Jiangxi Lianhe Mining, and is now officially in partnership with Nordic.)[16] There have been reports of a proposed US$2 billion project for iron-ore production in Isua, near Nuup Kangerlua, to be pursued by London Mining with Chinese state-owned corporation Xinye Mining backing, but it is unclear what the progress on this project has been. One report claims that it has yet to be approved, owing to Chinese concerns that the December 2012 'large-scale law' may be repealed or amended by the new government.[17] But London Mining suggested in June 2013 that while it is 'in preliminary discussions regarding the financing of [the] Isua project ... it is not currently in discussions with state-owned mining firm Sichuan Xinue [sic] Mining'.[18]

Greenland is not the only Arctic territory that has attracted interest from Chinese investors. Iceland rejected a proposal from Chinese businessman and former CCP International Department division head Huang Nubo for the purchase of 300km^2 of land on the island to develop an ecotourism centre.[19] The development plan was viewed with great suspicion, given its chosen location – the desolate Grímsstadir in northeastern Iceland – and the fanciful notion of a golf course. Iceland's minister for the interior who rejected the plan, Ogmundur Jónasson, was quoted as saying that 'it never seemed a very convincing plan … One has to look at this from a geopolitical perspective and ask about motivations.'[20] Huang reportedly remains eager to lease the land on a 40-year deal, despite the purchase being rejected.

The issue of geopolitics raised by Jónasson, and the slightly overblown fears that Grímsstadir could become a clandestine Chinese military air base, naval facility or signals-intelligence centre, reflect the regional concerns over China's increasing interest in the region. The first visit by a Chinese leader to Iceland in 40 years occurred when then-Premier Wen Jiabao arrived in April 2012; this was closely followed by a port call to Reykjavik by the Chinese icebreaker *Xuelong*, in July 2012, after its first trans-Arctic crossing. One month earlier, Hu Jintao had paid the first visit to Denmark by a Chinese head of state in history. The fact that these diplomatic engagements were taking place in the two countries in which Chinese companies appeared most eager to invest underlined the potential political importance of the industrial decisions. It also seemed to suggest that Beijing was attempting to develop greater soft power and economic influence over the weaker members of the Arctic club: Iceland, a small country that had recently undergone a crippling financial crisis, and Greenland, an autonomous territory of just 57,000 people desperate for foreign investment. It is no coincidence that, in April 2013, Iceland became the first European country to sign a free-trade agreement with China.[21]

China has already expressed an interest in greater involvement in the Arctic: it has been an ad hoc observer on the Arctic Council since 2007 and was accepted as a permanent observer in 2013. Moreover, it has a significant Arctic research budget: it has conducted five maritime research expeditions, and founded its first Arctic research station, named Huanghe, at Ny-Alesund in Svalbard in 2004.[22] A second Chinese icebreaker to complement the Ukraine-built *Xuelong* is expected to be completed by 2014.[23] China's Polar Research Institute announced its intention to establish a China–Nordic Arctic Research Centre in Shanghai in mid-2013.[24]

The reasons for China's interest in the Arctic are obvious: the potential for resource wealth to power its growing and hungry economy; the possibility of shorter trading routes to Europe; and the impact of Arctic warming on weather and precipitation patterns in Northeast Asia. However, Arctic states have been concerned about the disturbing rhetoric, suggestive of a proprietary and meddlesome atmosphere in Chinese thinking, which has at times accompanied this interest. In 2009, renowned Chinese Arctic commentator Guo Peiqing noted that China should not 'stay out of Arctic affairs', while Rear Admiral Yin Zhuo, who previously had suggested that China should establish military bases in the Middle East, stated that 'China must play an indispensable role in Arctic exploration as we have one fifth of the world's population,' and 'the North Pole and the sea area around the North Pole belong to all the people of the world.'[25] While these statements are neither aggressive nor factually inaccurate (the large area of the Arctic Ocean beyond the 200nm EEZs are high seas available for exploitation by anyone), they have unnerved Arctic states, particularly given China's increasingly assertive policies in the South and East China seas in recent years. No Chinese official has endorsed such rhetoric, and it appears to have receded since 2010. Nevertheless, there is now a trend in Chinese semi-official discourse to note its status as a 'near-Arctic state', a fact that highlights China's continued political interest in the Arctic.[26]

Concerns over China's intentions in the Arctic have manifested in the failure of a previous unsuccessful bid by Beijing to become a permanent observer on the Arctic Council in 2009. In addition, Beijing's relations with Arctic states have not always been ideal: the strategic partnership with and simultaneous mistrust of and by Russia, and the growing strategic competition with the US, are well known. However, Norway and China have also had their points of discord. In 2010, when the Nobel Peace Prize was awarded (by a committee appointed by the Norwegian parliament) to the detained Chinese activist Liu Xiaobo, Beijing reacted angrily. Restrictions were placed on Norwegian salmon imports, Norway was omitted from a list of 45 countries whose citizens could enjoy 72-hour visa-free access to Beijing, and former Norwegian prime minister Kjell Magne Bondevik was denied a visa in mid-2012.[27] While the sanctions were light, the Sino-Norwegian spat was a further example of how geopolitics can intrude in and be influenced by the Arctic sphere.

Northeast Asia and Europe

China's desire to be viewed as an Arctic state is not unique in Northeast Asia. Japan and South Korea were also accepted as permanent observers on the Arctic Council in 2013, and both have histories of Arctic research and maintain scientific stations in Svalbard. With healthy export sectors and fishing and shipping industries, both are interested in the potential for fish resources and especially shorter trade routes to Europe (the first LNG tanker to complete a trans-Arctic journey, the *Ob River*, did so travelling from Norway to Japan).[28] South Korea has already invested in energy resources in the Arctic: in 2011 the state-run Korea Gas Corporation announced a US$30.1 million purchase of a 20% stake in a Canadian Arctic gas field (the Umiak block) in the Mackenzie Delta.[29] Both countries have also engaged in Arctic research for several years: South Korea established the Dasan Station at Ny-Alesund in 2002; Japan's National Institute of Polar Research established a Ny-Alesund observation station in 1991. However, neither country has a presence beyond research and commerce: Japan's military icebreaker, the *Shirase*, operates solely in Antarctic waters, usually in support of whaling fleets. South Korea's government-operated icebreaker, *Araon*, commissioned in 2010, has already launched seven Arctic and Antarctic missions, with its latest being to the Chukchi and Beaufort seas in August 2013.[30] There are fewer concerns among the Arctic states about both South Korean and Japanese involvement in the region, though, perhaps because their presence is not supported by ambiguous statements in state-run press and by government-affiliated commentators. Indeed, the addition of South Korea and Japan as permanent observers on the Arctic Council was ostensibly to reflect their Arctic research, presence and potential influence as markets for resources, but could equally be seen as an attempt to balance China's acceptance as an observer with a presence from other Asian states.

European states have also been active in the Arctic and have sought greater influence in the north. Seven of the 12 permanent observers are European states, including France, Germany, the Netherlands, Poland, Spain, the UK and Italy (the latter was accepted in 2013). Again, the European observer applications have not been seen to be as contentious as China's, but equally there was disquiet about the expansion of the organisation to include many more countries. As the International Institute for Strategic Studies (IISS) noted after the 2013 Kiruna meeting,

> The indigenous permanent participants were concerned about being edged out of their central role in the discussion about activities in their territory. Nordic countries were largely supportive of opening up the Council to more observers, but Russia and Canada feared that the

primacy of Arctic states in Arctic affairs could be weakened.[31]

One significant change to the geopolitical landscape that is likely to occur in the near future is the acceptance of the EU as an Arctic Council observer. The EU has already signalled its interest in the Arctic (see, for example, the 2008 Communication from the Commission to the European Parliament and Council on the Arctic) and three of the eight Arctic states are EU members (Iceland is a candidate state and could become the fourth). The EU therefore already has a presence of sorts in the north, even if its Arctic members have by and large preferred to act unilaterally rather than through Brussels. The organisation has already devised a 'Northern Dimension' between itself, Russia, Norway and Iceland that seeks to promote dialogue, economic cooperation and integration, and is a member of the Barents Euro-Arctic Council, alongside the Nordic Arctic countries and Russia. The EU's bid to join as an observer was rejected in 2013, owing to Canadian indigenous groups' grievances over an EU seal-products import ban, but this is likely to be resolved in the near future.[32] A more active EU role in the Arctic has the potential to rebalance the geopolitical role that each state currently plays, theoretically adding support to Arctic EU states' positions, creating a more cohesive European policy and fuelling further mistrust in Moscow about the meddling of Western-centric organisations. For now, the low-key approach of the EU to the matter has prevented such an outcome, but in the medium term the European organisation's intervention, and that of the near-Arctic European states, could shift the balance of power within the region.

The Arctic in a global context

The inclusion of Northeast Asian and European countries as observers on the Arctic Council could reflect their geographical location near the Arctic. Yet those countries with an interest in the region extend far beyond the near-Arctic. India and Singapore were also admitted as observers to the council at its 2013 meeting.

These two countries' interest in the region reflects the global effects that a changing Arctic may have, particularly in the realm

Indigenous groups

One aspect of Arctic politics is often overlooked: the role of indigenous groups. This is peculiar because, theoretically, the six indigenous groups that are permanent participants on the Arctic Council have a greater role to play in the forum's deliberations than do observer states such as China and the UK. Permanent participants have full consultation rights on the negotiations and decisions of the council, although they are not decision-making members themselves.

The six groups (the Arctic Athabaskan Council; Aleut International Association; Gwich'in Council International; Inuit Circumpolar Council; Russian Association of Indigenous Peoples of the North; and the Saami Council) seem, at first glance, to be an unequivocally positive addition to the council. The addition of indigenous peoples' organisations should ensure representation of the otherwise marginalised communities, and encourage greater interaction with populations in isolated parts of the world.

However, even the indigenous world has not been free from politicking and major-power machinations. At the 7th Russian Association of Indigenous Peoples of the North (RAIPON) Congress in March 2013, an election was held to determine the next president. Leading after two ballots was the deputy president Pavel Sulyandziga, a strong proponent of indigenous rights and an occasional opponent of the exploitation of local resources. However, Sulyandziga withdrew his candidacy mysteriously after the second round, leaving the second-placed candidate, Gregory Ledkov, who also happens to be State Duma deputy for President Putin's party, United Russia, to take the third-round vote. Delegates present at the vote raised suspicions that pressure may have been placed on Sulyandziga to withdraw in favour of Moscow's preferred candidate.[34] The election occurred less than five months after Moscow had ordered the temporary closure of RAIPON for failing to align its statutes with federal law – a threat that drew statements of concern from the Arctic Council, which were approved by the Russian delegation.[35] This demonstrates the political importance of indigenous groups as further potential barriers to resource exploitation.

of shipping and trade. Singapore, in particular, is concerned that the development of a viable Arctic trade route may undermine its own position as a major entrepôt, and the city-state has had an Arctic special envoy since January 2012.[33] India, meanwhile, has had an Arctic research station in Svalbard (the Himadri Station) since 2008, and is a country that could be substantially affected by shifts in trade routes, as well as climate change and sea-level rises.

Their presence as observers may not yet affect the politics of the council or the region more broadly, but it underlines the increasing globalisation of the Arctic. This, in turn, will have an impact on the way that Arctic states interact with each other and the wider world, either seeking greater extra-regional interest for investment, or attempting to reject it to ensure that contentious issues such as the status of the NWP are not elevated to the global stage.

This process of geopolitical change, driven by geographical change in the Arctic, is under way and its outcome is not yet certain. It is, however, much like the retreat of the sea ice, currently irreversible. The changes in the Arctic are already engendering a more active Russia in the region, opening its north to exploitation and, potentially military, activity. Regional geopolitics is also evolving, with the Nordic and North American countries developing different strategic approaches to the Arctic. And finally, non-Arctic states are increasingly playing a role in shaping the agenda (if not actually the policies) of the region.

Geopolitical change is therefore afoot in the Arctic. As with all politics, there are elements of competition as states attempt to further their self-interest, but by and large it has been collaborative and focused on the mutual benefits to be gained. This theme is likely to continue. Meanwhile, the various states' soft and political power is already adapting to the changes, and the way in which politics is fashioned in the region will undergo a transformation.

Notes

1 Prime Minister's Office, 'Finland's Strategy for the Arctic Region', 5 July 2010, http://www.geopoliticsnorth.org/images/stories/attachments/Finland.pdf; Security Council of the Russian Federation, 'Osnovy gosudarstvennoy politiki Rossiyskoy Federatsii v Arktike na period do 2020 goda i dalneyshuyu perspektivu', 18 September 2008, http://www.scrf.gov.ru/documents/98.html; 'National Security Presidential Directive 66' and 'Homeland Security Presidential Directive 25', 9 January 2009, http://georgewbush-whitehouse.archives.gov/news/releases/2009/01/20090112-3.html; USCG, 'United States Coast Guard Arctic Strategy', May 2013, http://www.uscg.mil/seniorleadership/DOCS/CG_Arctic_Strategy.pdf; Ministry of Indian Affairs and Northern Development, 'Canada's Northern Strategy: Our North, Our Heritage, Our Future', 2009, http://www.northernstrategy.gc.ca/cns/cns-eng.asp; Speech by Stefan Füle, 'European Union strategy for the Arctic', 17 April 2013, http://europa.eu/rapid/press-release_SPEECH-13-329_en.htm; Danish, Faroese and Greenlandic ministries of foreign affairs, 'Kingdom of Denmark Strategy for the Arctic 2011–2020', August 2011, http://um.dk/en/~/media/UM/English-site/Documents/Politics-and-diplomacy/Arktis_Rapport_UK_210x270_Final_Web.ashx; Norwegian Ministry of Foreign Affairs, 'The Norwegian Government's High North Strategy', 2006, http://www.regjeringen.no/upload/UD/Vedlegg/strategien.pdf; Norwegian Ministry of Foreign Affairs, 'Nye byggesteiner i nord', 2009, http://www.regjeringen.no/upload/UD/Vedlegg/Nordomr%C3%A5dene/byggesteiner_nord090323_2.pdf. The US defence department's Arctic strategy, released in November 2013, sets out the Pentagon's role in meeting the broad priorities of the national strategy; see US Department of Defense, 'Arctic Strategy', November 2013.

2 This analysis is based on Lassi Heininen, *Arctic Strategies and Policies: Inventory and comparative study* (Akureyri: Northern Research Forum/University of Lapland Press, 2011).

3 Halford J. Mackinder, 'The geographical pivot of history', *The Geographical Journal*, vol. 23, no. 4, April 1904, pp. 421–43.

4 Alfred Thayer Mahan, *The Influence of Sea Power Upon History, 1660–1783* (London: Sampson Low and Co., 1890).

5 Nicholas J. Spykman, *The Geography of the Peace* (New York: Harcourt, Bruce and Co., 1944).

6 Zbigniew Brzezinski, *The Grand Chessboard: American Primacy and Its Geostrategic Imperatives* (New York: Basic Books, 1997).

7 Robert D. Kaplan, *Monsoon: The Indian Ocean and the Future of American Power* (New York: Random House, 2010).

8 MacArthur Foundation, 'Arctic Funders' Group Consultation – Web/Executive Summary', http://www.macfound.org/media/files/Russian_Arctic_Consultation_-_Exec_Summary.pdf.

9   Caitlyn L. Antrim, 'The Next Geographical Pivot: The Russian Arctic in the Twenty-First Century', *Naval War College Review*, vol. 63, no. 3, Summer 2010, pp. 15–37.

10 Helga Haftendorn, 'NATO and the Arctic: Is the Atlantic alliance a Cold War relic in a peaceful region now faced with non-military challenges?', *European Security*, vol. 20, no. 3, p. 341.

11 'The Ilulissat Declaration', Arctic Ocean Conference, 27–9 May 2008, http://www.oceanlaw.org/downloads/arctic/Ilulissat_Declaration.pdf.

12 Sven-Ronald Nystø, 'Governance in the Arctic – Sharing Best Practices – Indigenous Peoples', paper delivered to the Wilton Park Conference 'The High North: Challenges and Opportunities', 18–20 February 2010.

13 'Arctic "five" discuss regional cooperation', *Voice of Russia*, 30 March 2010.

14 'Mining proponents win Greenland election', Associated Press, 13 March 2013.

15 'Greenland passes mining projects bill, opens for cheap labor', Reuters, 7 December 2012.

16 MINEX, 'Greenland Mineral Exploration Newsletter', October 2012, http://www.geus.dk/minex/minex42.pdf; 'Jiangxi enterprises to enter world's largest mine', *Jiangxi News*, 9 June 2009.

17 Carol Matlack, 'Chinese workers – in Greenland?', Bloomberg Businessweek, 10 February 2013; Jun Pu, 'Greenland lures China's miners with cold gold', *Caixin*, 7 December 2011.

18 Stephen Blank, 'China's Arctic strategy', *Diplomat*, 20 June 2013.

19 Linda Jakobson and Jingchao Peng, 'China's Arctic aspirations', SIPRI Policy Paper 34, November 2012, p. 9.

20 Andrew Higgins, 'Teeing off at edge of the Arctic? A Chinese plan baffles Iceland', *New York Times*, 22 March 2013.

21 Omar R. Vladimarsson, 'Iceland is first in Europe to sign free trade pact with China', Bloomberg, 15 April 2013.

22 Trude Pettersen, 'Chinese icebreaker concludes Arctic voyage', *Barents Observer*, 27 September 2012; Linda Jakobson, 'China prepares for an ice-free Arctic', *SIPRI Insights on Peace and Security*, no. 2, March 2010.

23 'China's 2nd icebreaker scheduled for use in 2014', *China Daily*, 9 April 2012.

24 Zhenghua Wang, 'China to build research center for Arctic region', *China Daily*, 6 June 2013.

25 Linda Jakobson and Jingchao Peng, 'China's Arctic aspirations', p. 15.

26 Gwynn Guilford, 'What is China's Arctic game plan?', *Atlantic*, 16 May 2013.

27 'Did China snub Norway in revenge over Liu Xiaobo Nobel Peace Prize?', *South China Morning Post*, 7 December 2012; Kristoffer Rønneberg, 'Kjell Magne Bondevik nektet visum til Kina', *Aftenposten*, 12 June 2012.

28 'LNG tanker from Norway arrives in Japan for the first time via Arctic route', *Xinhua*, 5 December 2012.

29 'South Korea to buy stakes in Canada gas field', *News*, 21 January 2011.

30 'S Korea's icebreaker departs for Arctic Ocean', KBS, 5 August 2013.

31 'Growing importance of the Arctic Council', IISS *Strategic Comments*, vol. 23, no. 16, 6 June 2013.

32 *Ibid.*

33 Mia Bennett, 'A look at East Asian diplomacy in the Arctic', *Alaska Dispatch*, 8 July 2013.

34 Thomas Nilsen, 'Moscow staged RAIPON election thriller', *Barents Observer*, 3 April 2013.

35 Atle Staalesen, 'Crackdown on RAIPON spurs international concern', *Barents Observer*, 15 November 2012.

CHAPTER SIX

The future of Arctic governance

Despite its significant (if conditional) economic potential, the unresolved sovereign status of much of the region and the geopolitical stakes, the Arctic is currently a zone of relatively low tension. Although conflicts and disputes exist, they are for the most part being addressed in a spirit of cooperation rather than confrontation. But this process is taking place in an evolving political and legal environment, and whether it can be sustained depends on whether and how Arctic governance is developed and strengthened as the region becomes increasingly accessible.

The post-Cold War Arctic, as a zone of peace and cooperation, was inaugurated by Soviet leader Mikhail Gorbachev in a seminal speech in Murmansk in October 1987.[1] The North, he said, was a problem for Soviet security: 'the people of Murmansk remember well the years 1918–1919 and 1941–1945.' While noting that some of the groundbreaking agreements and meetings that pointed towards the end of Cold War tensions – the Helsinki Accords, the 1986 Stockholm Document, the 1986 Reykjavik Summit – had taken place in northern capitals, he warned that 'the militarization of this part of the world is assuming threatening dimensions.' He proposed six concrete solutions: a nuclear-free zone in Northern Europe; scaling down of and restrictions on military activity in

the Baltic, Northern, Norwegian and Greenland seas; cooperation in developing the economic and resource potential of the
Arctic, including the Soviet Union's continental shelf; setting
up a joint Arctic Research Council; developing an integrated,
comprehensive international plan for environmental protection
in the region; and opening the NSR to foreign shipping, with
the Soviet Union providing icebreaker support. The polar and
sub-polar regions should become 'a genuine zone of peace and
fruitful cooperation', he said.

With the exception of the nuclear-free zone, significant
progress was made in all these areas in the subsequent quarter-
century. Although traffic on the NSR actually peaked in the year
of Gorbachev's speech, the route was opened to foreign shipping
by the Soviet Union in 1991. The call for international scientific
and environmental cooperation led directly to the precursors of
the Arctic Council, and eventually to the council itself. Almost
all hydrocarbon exploration and production in Arctic waters
– Western as well as Russian – has been through multinational energy companies or joint ventures. And, as discussed in
Chapter Three, military activity, both naval and aerial, declined
in the Arctic, although this was due to the lessening of East–West
tensions globally and to the crisis within the Russian military
rather than to any concrete agreements. Joint training and
exercises, and other confidence-building measures mooted by
Gorbachev in his speech, however, have multiplied.

Russia is the key Arctic nation, both in terms of its territorial
extent and population within the region, and (with the exception
of Greenland and Iceland, which lie entirely within the wider
Arctic) the relative importance of the region to its economy as a
whole. By these metrics, among the coastal states, the Arctic is of
least importance to the United States, a situation reflected in the
slower development of a US Arctic strategy, of operational capabilities and of representation in international forums, compared
to the other Arctic nations.

Despite an apparent hardening of Russian attitudes in many areas of international relations in recent years, at least on a rhetorical level, President Vladimir Putin has echoed Gorbachev's call for the Arctic to be a 'zone of peace and cooperation'[2] (although statements from a variety of Russian policymakers equally often play up the potential threat from foreign powers in the Arctic, and even Putin has highlighted the fact that 'flight times of the [US ballistic] missiles from that area [off northern Norway's coast] to Moscow is some 16–17 minutes').[3] And although Russia, Canada and the US all make sovereignty and national security a priority in their respective national Arctic strategies, they all place equal weight on economic development, environmental protection and governance – in keeping with the consensus that emerges from the policy statements of all eight Arctic states. As Arctic states with significant populations and resources in the region, but no Arctic coastline, Finland and Sweden have a narrower focus on economic and environmental issues, and tend to stress human development more than most of the others do.

Russia has a strong interest in maintaining the Arctic as a zone of peace; its economic opportunities are so great in both absolute and relative terms that they outweigh other security considerations. This is reflected by the 2010 Russian–Norwegian maritime boundary agreement, its quick ratification by the Russian parliament and the rapid expansion of hydrocarbon exploration into the previously disputed areas, after 40 years of negotiations. Moreover, Russia requires huge foreign investment and partnerships with multinational companies in order to develop its Arctic territory and resources. A stable Arctic, governed by the rule of law, is desirable for all concerned.

Yet the rule of law requires not just statutes and structures, such as UNCLOS, but also effective dispute-resolution and enforcement mechanisms, and a readiness of all parties to use them and abide by the results. In this respect, the Arctic is by no means in anarchy, but the governance structure of the region is nascent and malleable.[4] A range of suggestions, from steps to guide the evolution of multi-level Arctic governance in different directions to the creation of a new, comprehensive international treaty regime, have been mooted.

An Arctic treaty?

Given the environmental fragility of the Arctic, and perceptions about resources, conflict and lack of governance, there has been international pressure to expand the governance of the Arctic to a wider group of stakeholders. Analysts in East and South Asia tend to argue for the Arctic as a global commons.[5] Calls for negotiation of an Arctic treaty analogous to the 50-year-old Antarctic Treaty System have come from several quarters.[6] Notable among these is a resolution adopted by the European Parliament in 2008.[7]

The 1961 Antarctic Treaty bans any permanent military presence on land and ice shelves south of 60°S, and establishes freedom of scientific investigation, with provisions for sharing of plans, results and personnel, and for inspection of facilities. It does not deal with pre-existing territorial claims, but puts them in abeyance and prohibits new claims or activities asserting, supporting or denying existing claims while the treaty is in force. Thus, no nation has sovereignty in Antarctica, and a large part of the continent remains unclaimed. Law enforcement and legal systems are the responsibility of nations undertaking activities in Antarctica, and individuals are subject to the jurisdiction of their country of citizenship. Through its provisions for frequent consultation, the treaty has led to a large number of subsidiary agreements and binding treaties, one of the most important of which is the Protocol on Environmental Protection, which came into force in 1998. Among other provisions, it prohibits any activity related to mineral resources other than scientific research. If this article is to be modified or rescinded at a review conference allowed for after 2048, it must include a binding legal regime that includes an agreed mechanism for determining when and how such activities could be carried out.[8]

The Antarctic model appeals most to the peripheral Arctic stakeholders, such as European and Asian maritime powers without Arctic territory or potential claims of their own, and to non-governmental organisations with an environmental or sustainable-development focus. But the applicability of the Antarctic model has even been questioned by some who want strict environmental controls and limits on activity in the Arctic.

The sovereignty issues in the two polar regions are different: Antarctica involves multiple, overlapping territorial claims and large areas of *terra nullius*, while disputes over land and terri- torial maritime boundaries in the Arctic are relatively minor. The issues in the North stem from real or potential claims for extended continental shelves and EEZs, while the Antarctic Treaty regime does not deal with maritime territory at all.[9] These conflicts are bilateral or, at worst, trilateral, so there is no pressing need for any dispute-resolution mechanisms outside UNCLOS. Finally, Antarctica is a polar continent surrounded by ocean; the Arctic is a polar sea surrounded by land. Thus, the environmental dynamics and potential impacts from activities within and outside the region will differ significantly.

Beyond that, the current circumstances of rapid environmen- tal change in the Arctic compared to Antarctica – either at the time the treaty was first established or as projected for the rest of this century – suggest that a comprehensive, binding treaty regime may not be a viable solution. While such an outcome may be desirable, it may not be achievable in practice, due to the complexities of negotiating and ratifying such broad agree- ments; the relative inflexibility of the resulting regimes; and the perennial stumbling block of dispute resolution and enforce- ment.[10] More to the point, such a regime would require not just the agreement, but the active involvement and support, of the five Arctic littoral states, all of which have rejected the idea, including collectively through the Ilulissat Declaration, and have no national economic or security interests in such a major step. The Protocol on Environmental Protection in Antarctica was negotiated to replace an earlier accord, signed by 19 nations (including six of the eight Arctic states) but not ratified by any, which would have allowed mining under arrangements similar to those under UNCLOS and the ISA for the high-seas area. That issue has been the principal stumbling block to US ratification of UNCLOS, and it is unlikely that any of the A5, particularly the US, would accept it beyond the parts of the Arctic Ocean acknowledged to be international waters.

Nevertheless, the Arctic is not isolated physically or politically, and the desires of the A5, or the A8, to keep Arctic governance in their own hands may be difficult to sustain in the face of pressure from other actors, such as the EU or China.[11] But among the criteria for accrediting new observers to the Arctic Council, adopted at its ministerial meeting in 2011, are the extent to which applicants 'recognize Arctic States' sovereignty, sovereign rights and jurisdiction in the Arctic' and 'recognize that an extensive legal framework applies to the Arctic Ocean including, notably, the Law of the Sea, and that this framework provides a solid foundation for responsible management of this ocean'.[12] Other criteria include demonstration of Arctic interest and expertise, and it is notable that the six European states given observer status before the expansion in 2013 – the United Kingdom, Germany, France, the Netherlands, Poland and Spain – all rank among the top-12 non-Arctic states in terms of Arctic scientific research, as do three of the new observers.[13]

Despite initial worries that the Ilulissat Declaration from the A5 would undermine the status of the A8 and hence the Arctic Council, it has in fact had the opposite effect.[14] That the council accepted China, India, Japan, South Korea, Singapore and Italy as observers in 2013, and looked favourably on the EU application, suggests likewise that the Arctic states do not see the formal or implied policies of these actors as obstacles to the current functioning or intended expansion of the council's role. On the contrary, the functioning of the Arctic Council is strengthened rather than weakened by the interest and participation of such actors.

Environmental security and governance

Despite the popular national-security narrative of dangerous disputes over territory and resources, the principal focus of diplomatic activity and the evolution of governance architecture in the Arctic has in fact been on broader issues of human and environmental security, and sustainable development. This is to be expected, since most of the developments that may give rise to security threats, as they are traditionally conceived, are environmental. These include first-order effects, as regional warming and other climatic changes affect ecosystems, and second-order effects due to the impacts of changing economic activity enabled or stimulated by the first-order changes. Political and military disputes are third-order effects, and may be dampened or diverted by successful policies in the first two realms.[15]

The Arctic is a bellwether and linchpin of global human and environmental security: it is warming faster than the rest of the planet, and this warming has critical effects on climate patterns well beyond the region. Its ecosystems and indigenous cultures are also particularly sensitive to the changing climate, and to pollution from activities within and outside the region. Global warming both directly increases environmental stress on the Arctic and creates openings for greater human activity that will have chronic environmental impacts and intensify the risk and severity of the acute effects of oil spills, industrial accidents and incidents involving merchant shipping and tourist vessels.

Although UNCLOS is acknowledged as the overarching legal framework governing the Arctic Ocean for environmental protection as well as territorial issues, it effectively serves as a constitution – a framework and set of legal guidelines – rather than explicit rules and regulations for governance of the world's oceans. In the environmental realm, national legal codes apply in territorial waters and EEZs, enforceable by military or paramilitary forces, but these codes must be at least as strict as internationally agreed rules, standards and practices for the high seas. And specific legal regimes are normally established on a regional basis, taking into account characteristic regional features.[16] Most parts of the world, with the notable exceptions of South, East and Northeast Asia, have marine environmental-protection conventions and protocols in place, with up to nine overlapping and complementary agreements in some cases.[17] Yet despite the Ilulissat Declaration, no such regional regime yet exists for the Arctic. The point of the declaration was, firstly, to establish that no new overarching treaty was necessary to create the rule of law in the region. This has now become the accepted wisdom. But the declaration was also an assertion that the competent actors for creating the specific rules and standards were the A5, which has met with less approbation.

Although there is a trend towards region-specific national legislation among the Arctic states, such as rules for navigation in the NSR (Russia) and the NWP (Canada), this is still the exception rather than the rule.[18] The 2011 Arctic search-and-rescue (SAR) cooperation treaty and the 2013 Arctic oil-pollution preparedness cooperation treaty are important not only in and of themselves, but as models and building blocks for an integrated governance regime such as those found in other seas and regions. Both were negotiated under the auspices of the Arctic Council and signed by all eight Arctic states; the SAR agreement has been ratified by all eight, and came into force in January 2013. But there are still important gaps. In particular, ship operations in the Arctic are governed by the general treaties and guidelines that establish global environmental and safety standards for shipping, notably the Safety of Life at Sea (SOLAS) Convention and the International

Convention for the Prevention of Pollution from Ships (known as MARPOL).[19] Over the last decade, the International Maritime Organization (IMO) has supplemented these conventions with recommended guidelines for ships operating in Arctic waters, taking into account the specific and extreme conditions encountered in the region.[20] These guidelines are non-mandatory; apply only to passenger and cargo ships larger than 500 tonnes and on international voyages; and exclude military, fishing and pleasure vessels. Since 2009, the IMO has been working on a mandatory Polar Code, although the initial target date for completion of 2012 has already slipped to 2014, at the earliest. The code is intended to cover design, construction, equipment, operational, training, search-and-rescue and environmental protection matters in both Arctic and Antarctic waters.[21] Agreement on such a code will be an important step for environmental security, as well as for a stable legal environment – a critical element for the economic viability of any expansion of Arctic shipping, particularly through the NSR.

Since Washington acknowledges much of the general framework provided by UNCLOS as customary international law, and through the Ilulissat Declaration specifically recognises its primacy in the Arctic, US failure to ratify the convention is not a real barrier to the development of an environmental-security regime made up of multiple instruments and multiple layers of governance. From a practical political perspective, too, it is easier to get any number of specific, narrowly focused agreements through the US Senate than it is to ratify an umbrella treaty such as UNCLOS, even if it is only the specific treaties that actually impose constraints on sovereignty and freedom of action.

There are, however, some stumbling blocks to UNCLOS as a framework for Arctic governance beyond the environmental realm. There are differences, for example, in the interpretation of exactly what 'innocent passage' and 'transit passage' entail, and specific differences over whether parts of the NWP and the

NSR constitute internal waters, territorial waters or international straits. Both types of dispute involve issues outside the Arctic, and any resolution or agreement may have more to do with national interests in other parts of the world, especially insofar as the dialogue expands to include stakeholders other than the A5 or A8.

The Arctic is also more than the Arctic Ocean. Land-based activity can have a significant impact on the fragile maritime environment in the region, so even an environmentally focused governance structure would have to cover the entire region to be effective. And there is a human factor: most Arctic states have substantial indigenous populations with unique political and cultural relations to the metropole. Against the pressure to develop region-wide governance structures and instruments, there is a countervailing trend, internationally and in many of the Arctic states, towards devolution of governance and increased recognition of the rights of indigenous peoples. The tension between the two is a significant complicating factor within several Arctic countries, and creates international difficulties when it raises human-rights issues.

The future of the Arctic Council

The May 2013 ministerial meeting of the Arctic Council in Kiruna was something of an inflection point for the forum. Symbolically, it marked the end of the council's adolescence. The handover from Sweden to Canada completed the first 16-year cycle in which each of the eight member states had held the chair in turn. A budget for the new permanent secretariat to support the work of the council was approved. The number of non-Arctic nations admitted as observers was doubled, including non-European states for the first time and bringing the proportion of the world's population represented in the forum to over 50%.

The council agreed a 'Vision for the Arctic' to guide its work over the next two decades. That document, the Kiruna

Declaration, issued at the end of the meeting, and the expressed plans for the Canadian chairmanship indicate the beginning of a shift in focus from environmental issues to human and economic development.[22] More important than this shift, which is more of a change of emphasis among issues and spheres that have been part of the council's competence since its inception than a step change, is the aspiration to 'expand the Arctic Council's roles from policy-shaping into policy-making'.[23] The negotiation of the SAR and oil-spill preparedness agreements under the auspices of the council reflect a strengthening policy-shaping role, but suggest the direction in which the forum could evolve. In the near term, the Kiruna Declaration outlines a number of initiatives that go beyond the detailed assessments and recommendations that have been the essence of the council's work to date. These include collaboration with the IMO on the development of its mandatory Polar Code, setting up a Circumpolar Business Forum and potential agreements on oil-pollution prevention and emissions reduction. Only the latter two matters are on a level with the two recent binding agreements.

For the Arctic Council to become a decision-making international organisation rather than an intergovernmental forum would require a formal Arctic convention of some sort. But this need not (indeed, probably could not) be the sort of global treaty and legal regime rejected in the Ilulissat Declaration; any such organisation would be a regional body, limited to the current membership of the council, presumably with a system of observers much like the current one. Its remit would be similar to that of the current forum; it would not claim jurisdiction over those parts of the Arctic that are global commons under UNCLOS. But there are some practical difficulties to the development and adoption of such a regime. Firstly, it would likely weaken the representation and influence of pan-national and transnational indigenous organisations. The presence on the council of six of these as permanent participants, with full consultation rights (but not voting rights), is a unique aspect of the Arctic Council and would be unlikely to survive a transition to a formal international organisation. Yet any diminishment of the role of the indigenous peoples in Arctic policy discussions would be a retrograde step that could defeat the purpose of a strengthened council, or stymie the adoption of a new, formal council charter. Secondly, domestic politics and opinion in some council-member states would make anything that appeared to constrain sovereign rights in the Arctic difficult to ratify, as the history of UNCLOS demonstrates.

Thirdly, there is the question of practical logistics. Meetings of the council and its working groups normally, and understandably, take place in Arctic communities, yet the limited transportation, accommodation, and conference and meeting facilities in such locales are often strained by the number of participants, observers and support staff. This will only be exacerbated by an increase in the number of observers accredited to the council, a factor that has been cited in the reluctance of some member states to expand the list. Many of the states granted observer status in 2013 had been waiting for many years, and no additional non-state applications were approved. Moreover, participation of many of the council members, permanent participants and observers in the important, detailed work of the various task forces and working groups of the council is already hampered by budgetary and human-resource constraints.

One of the strengths of the Arctic Council so far has been the small, intimate and informal nature of the ministerial gathering, along with the relative remoteness of the meetings, which tends to keep them out of the media spotlight. Paradoxically, however, as international interest in the region and in the work of the Arctic Council expands, strengthening the council's role as a normative body requires raising its profile.

To this end, in 2012 the council adopted a formal communications strategy, intended to provide continuity of message across the council, its working groups and the member states, and between chairmanships.[24] Its target audience includes local, regional, national and international policymakers, as well as inhabitants of the Arctic; NGOs; the scientific and research community, the business community; and the media. Its principal long-term aim is to ensure that the council is 'perceived as the pre-eminent forum for international cooperation in the Arctic'. This is to be done through a number of key messages: the council is the most prominent, credible and relevant forum for Arctic issues; it provides for participation of indigenous peoples in decision-making; it works to ensure environmental preservation and sustainable development of natural resources; and it addresses the need for adaptation and resilience to climate change. What is notable is not that a communications strategy exists – any organisation hoping to shape or create public policy needs one. The significance lies in the fact that the council had no such centralised and coordinated strategy for the first 15 years of its existence. The new strategy, in conjunction with the creation of a permanent secretariat to implement it, is an important step in the evolution of the council. Moreover, the work of the council is hindered by the popular view of Arctic competition and confrontation, and the new communications strategy could help to change the narrative.

If a new, formal Arctic convention, either modelled on the Antarctic Treaty System or limited to the Arctic Council member states, is unlikely to emerge, it is still unclear how far along the continuum from a talking shop to a formal organisation the council will be permitted or able to develop, and how it will get there. Whatever new structure emerges is unlikely to differ radically from other regional governance and security architectures elsewhere in the world. Although a stable and secure Arctic is an important goal, the global significance of Arctic governance will stem more from the process than the product: the way it emerges can be a model for other regions.

To the extent that UNCLOS remains the framework for Arctic governance, and the council remains the sort of regional body envisioned under UNCLOS to flesh out the agreement's 'constitutional' structure, the most important variable is whether the US will ratify the treaty. Failure to do so, however, is not an insurmountable roadblock to effective regional governance. The Mediterranean, for example, has a well-regulated regime of treaties and conventions on environmental and maritime safety, even though the region contains many mutually hostile countries and unresolved maritime-boundary disputes involving significant energy resources, especially in the Eastern Mediterranean, where Israel, Turkey and Syria all remain outside UNCLOS. Moreover, while US ratification of UNCLOS would certainly ease the path for development of the council as a policymaking body, it would only be a first step. In contrast to the situation in the Mediterranean, all the countries involved in disputes in the South China Sea are parties to UNCLOS (apart from Taiwan, which is excluded from UNCLOS as it lacks UN country status), yet that has not stopped the region from becoming one of the world's crisis spots.[25] With better inter-state relations in general, a history of cooperation and fewer boundary disputes, the Arctic is better placed to develop stable governance structures than many other parts of the world. The Arctic Council is unlikely to become an overarching governing organisation for the region, but rather is likely to serve as the central pillar of a multi-level, multi-instrument regime designed to ensure peace and stability.

Arctic security cooperation

To be effective, such a regime would have to include another pillar to cover security and defence cooperation, but the Arctic Council is unlikely to expand to cover such issues. The same reasons of expediency that led to their original exclusion from the council's remit will continue to stand in the way, and any attempt to expand that remit would be counterproductive and would slow the development of the council's influence and competence in other areas. In practical terms, moreover, grafting a new working group on defence and security onto the existing council structure would be difficult. The council's expertise, from the highest level to the working groups, has always been drawn from foreign, environmental and trade ministries, and the scientific and academic communities. Nor have individual member states or the council as a whole expressed much interest in such an extension. Expanding the remit to consider military and security issues would be incompatible with the aspiration to shift from a policy-shaping to a policymaking role.

There have been suggestions that Arctic defence and security cooperation could develop under the aegis of NATO, since four of the five coastal states are members and mechanisms already exist. However, there is little interest in such a role within NATO.[26] As a common Norwegian saying puts it, 'NATO's area extends to the North Pole, but Brussels's maps all stop at Oslo.' More importantly, given Russia's suspicion of NATO involvement, such a move risks importing problems in NATO–Russia relations from outside the region into the Arctic debate. As long as Moscow objects, promoting NATO as a framework for Arctic security is counterproductive. The Alliance does have a minor role to play in promoting Arctic stability through dampening down conflict between allies over bilateral disputes, as it has done in the cases of the UK–Iceland 'cod wars' and tensions between Greece and Turkey. However, this role depends, to an extent, on the importance of collective defence to the allies, and thus functions in inverse proportion to any potential role NATO could play in the Arctic involving cooperation with Russia.[27]

Security cooperation in the Arctic lags some two decades behind the political, economic and environmental cooperation exemplified by the Arctic Council. Nascent and ad hoc forums such as the Arctic chiefs-of-defence staff meetings and Arctic security-forces roundtables, along with greater constabulary collaboration, could form the kernel of a multi-level, multi-organisation security architecture similar to the emerging parallel system of Arctic governance, but there are a number of practical problems with this.[28] The work of the Arctic Council in overseeing the negotiations of the SAR and oil-spill response agreements is a step towards developing a security-cooperation structure. But given the sensitivities of defence issues and the overlap between military and constabulary roles in some of the Arctic nations, a regular, non-political and NGO-driven forum bringing together security actors and decision-makers with a broader range of experts, business and political leaders, and other stakeholders might enable and catalyse such cooperation.

World enough, and time

Swedish Foreign Minister Carl Bildt has noted that the Arctic Council represents an almost unique situation in international diplomacy, which he calls 'diplomacy ahead of the game'. The warming of the Arctic has been both expected and gradual. 'We know what's going to happen, and we're setting up in advance the framework and the structures and principles of cooperation and integration.'[29] But the Arctic is a moving target. The gradual, evolutionary development of a multi-instrument governance and security architecture for the Arctic threatens to be outstripped by the pace of environmental change in the region. At the most basic level, this is already happening in terms of the assessment reports on various aspects of the Arctic economy and environment. There are usually five or six years between major assessments, yet the pace of change is such that reports are sometimes obsolete even before they are published. To the extent that policymaking is informed and driven by such assessments, this is a significant problem.

This extends further into the political realm. The Arctic Council has been relatively efficient and able to keep up with developments but, if the pace of climate change accelerates, this may no longer be the case – especially as the evolution of the Arctic Council is likely to reduce, at least to some extent, the flexibility and adaptability it has shown in the past.

While the Arctic Council will still be more flexible and adaptable in keeping up with the changes taking place in the region than a more formal governance regime would be, its strengthening and expansion will have to be tempered by an acknowledgement of the uncertainties surrounding the nature and speed of climatic developments.[30] This may be hindered, to some extent, by domestic political posturing in most of the Arctic countries, especially Canada, Russia and the US, where the narrative of Arctic competition is particularly strong. This narrative may be wrong, but perception can create its own reality. In any case, this friction would likewise be greater in attempts to establish an overarching Arctic convention.

If it is not 'the only game in town', the Arctic Council is nevertheless the most likely foundation for an effective system of governance to enable peace and stability in the region. As it expands its base of observers, it can draw on increased expertise and resources while maintaining a consensus-based decision-making process limited to a narrow group of actors. The success of Arctic governance will depend on the degree to which the council is able to balance the interests of its members with those of other stakeholders; to manage its timely expansion and enhancement as an institution; and to facilitate and assimilate the parallel development of defence and security cooperation.[31]

Notes

[1] Mikhail Gorbachev, speech in Murmansk, 1 October 1987; ttp://www.barentsinfo.fi/docs/Gorbachev_speech.pdf. For an analysis of the speech, see Paul Arthur Berkman, *Environmental Security in the Arctic Ocean: Promoting co-operation and preventing conflict*, Whitehall Paper no. 75, Royal United Services Institute, 30 September 2010, pp. 52–5.

[2] See Chapter Three.

3   See Chapter Three and 'Putin: Arctic is an integral part of Russia', Barents Nova, 4 October 2013.

4   Protection of the Marine Environment Working Group, Arctic Council, *The Arctic Ocean Review: Phase I Report (2009–2011)* (Akureyri: PAME, 2011), http://www.aor.is/images/stories/AOR_Phase_I_Report_to_Ministers_2011.pdf.

5   Aki Tonami, 'Review: Arctic governance and Japan's foreign strategy', The Arctic Institute, http://www.thearcticinstitute.org/2013/04/review-arctic-governance-and-japans.html; Jayantha Dhanapala, 'The Arctic as a bridge', *Bulletin of the Atomic Scientists*, 4 February 2013, http://www.thebulletin.org/arctic-bridge.

6   See Ed Struzik, 'As the Far North melts, calls grow for Arctic treaty', environment360, 14 June 2010, http://e360.yale.edu/feature/as_the_far_north_melts_calls_grow_for_arctic_treaty/2281/.

7   European Parliament, 'Resolution of 9 October 2008 on Arctic governance', http://www.europarl.europa.eu/sides/getDoc.do?type=TA&language=EN&reference=P6-TA-2008-0474.

8   'Protocol on Environmental Protection to the Antarctic Treaty', 1998, http://www.ats.aq/documents/keydocs/vol_1/vol1_4_AT_Protocol_on_EP_e.pdf.

9   For more detailed discussion of some of these issues, see Oren R. Young, 'Arctic governance – pathways to the future', *Arctic Review on Law and Politics,* vol. 1, no. 2, 2010, pp. 164–85.

10 *Ibid.*, pp. 181–4.

11 *Ibid.*, pp. 169–73.

12 Arctic Council, 'Nuuk Declaration', 12 May 2011, http://www.arctic-council.org/index.php/en/document-archive/category/5-declarations; Arctic Council, 'Senior Arctic Officials' Report to the Ministers', May 2011, http://www.arctic-council.org/index.php/en/document-archive/category/20-main-documents-from-nuuk#.

13 Grégoire Côte and Michelle Picard-Aitken, *Arctic Research in Canada: A bibliometric analysis* (Montreal: Science-Metric, 2009).

14 See Anton Vasiliev, 'Is the Ilulissat Declaration adequate?', Arctic – Changing Realities Conference, Copenhagen, 26 May 2010, http://www.norden.org/en/nordic-council-of-ministers/ministers-for-co-operation-mr-sam/the-arctic/calender/arctic-changing-realities/speeches-and-presentations/anton-vasiliev-is-the-ilulissat-declaration-adequate.

15 For a discussion of first-, second- and third-order effects of climate change in general, see Paul E. Herman and Gregory F. Treverton, 'The political consequences of climate change', *Survival: Global Politics and Strategy*, vol. 51, no. 2, April–May 2009, pp. 137–47.

16 Timo Koivurova, 'Gaps in international regulatory frameworks for the Arctic Ocean', in Paul Arthur Berkman and Alexander N. Vylegzhanin (eds), *Environmental Security in the Arctic Ocean* (Dordrecht: Springer, 2010), pp. 147–9.

17 See United Nations Environment Programme website, http://www.unep.org/regionalseas/about/default.asp.

18 Sustainable Development Working Group, 'Arctic Human

Development Report II: Regional Processes & Global Linkages Fact Sheet', January 2013, MM08_AHDR_FactSheet_Jan_2013.pdf.

[19] International Maritime Organization, 'International Convention for the Safety of Life at Sea', 1974, http://www.imo.org/About/Conventions/ListOfConventions/Pages/International-Convention-for-the-Safety-of-Life-at-Sea-%28SOLAS%29,-1974.aspx; International Maritime Organization, 'International Convention for the Prevention of Pollution from Ships', http://www.imo.org/about/conventions/listofconventions/pages/international-convention-for-the-prevention-of-pollution-from-ships-%28marpol%29.aspx.

[20] IMO, 'Guidelines for Ships Operating in Arctic Ice Covered Waters', 23 December 2002; IMO, 'Guidelines for Ships Operating in Polar Waters', 2 December 2009, available at http://library.arcticportal.org/1475/.

[21] International Maritime Organization, 'Development of an international code of safety for ships operating in polar waters (Polar Code)', http://www.imo.org/MediaCentre/HotTopics/polar/Pages/default.aspx.

[22] 'Kiruna Declaration', Kiruna, 15 May 2013 and 'Vision for the Arctic', Kiruna, 15 May 2013, both available at http://www.arctic-council.org/index.php/en/document-archive/category/425-main-documents-from-kiruna-ministerial-meeting; 'Growing importance of the Arctic Council',

IISS Strategic Comments, vol. 19, no. 16, 6 June 2013, http://www.iiss.org/en/publications/strategic%20comments/sections/2013-a8b5/growing-importance-of-the-arctic-council-4132.

[23] 'Vision for the Arctic', p. 3.

[24] 'Kiruna Senior Arctic Officials' Report to Ministers', Kiruna, 15 May 2013, available at http://www.arctic-council.org/index.php/en/document-archive/category/425-main-documents-from-kiruna-ministerial-meeting.

[25] For a full discussion the South China Sea disputes and the role of UNCLOS, see Sarah Raine and Christian Le Mière, *Regional Disorder: The South China Sea Disputes* (Abingdon: Routledge for the IISS, 2013).

[26] See Chapter Four.

[27] For a detailed discussion of NATO's Arctic role, see Helga Haftendorn, 'NATO and the Arctic: is the Atlantic alliance a cold war relic in a peaceful region now faced with non-military challenges?', *European Security*, vol. 20, no. 3, September 2011, pp. 337–61.

[28] See discussion in Chapters One, Four and Five.

[29] IISS Forum for Arctic Climate Change and Security, Capstone Seminar, Stockholm, 19 April 2013, Final Report, available at http://www.iiss.org/en/events/events/archive/2013-5126/april-d2df/forum-for-arctic-climate-change-and-security-capstone-seminar-a8ad.

[30] Oren R. Young, 'Arctic tipping points – governance in turbulent times', *Ambio*, vol. 41, no. 1, February 2012, pp. 75–84.

CONCLUSION

One thing is certain in the Arctic: the region is undergoing fundamental change. It is unclear exactly how this change will affect the rate of decline in sea ice; future accessibility of resources and trade routes; or the nature of interactions between Arctic and non-Arctic actors.

This dichotomy between the certainty about the fact of climate change in the Arctic and the uncertainty over its future effects is causing differences of opinion and division. It is certain, for example, that there will be less ice and therefore greater economic exploitation. But governments, industry and indigenous groups have different opinions on the intensity and levels of regulation of private enterprise that are appropriate. It is certain that the future of the Arctic is no longer just a regional issue, but there are differences of opinion on where the Arctic sits in a global context. It is certain that governance will reform and evolve, but there are divisions over what governance there will be among the A5 themselves, between the A5 and A8, and even within some Arctic countries, such as Denmark and the autonomous territory of Greenland.

Perhaps most importantly, there is a level of certainty that there will be more activity in the Arctic, but a degree of uncertainty over whether it will be benign. Some commentators have focused on the possibility of confrontation, while policymakers almost uniformly highlight the potential for the Arctic to be a region of cooperation and law. While this *Adelphi* sketches out the reasons why cooperation is currently more likely than conflict, this is predicated on the development of further regional security architectures and does not preclude the possibility of geopolitical, non-military competition. Furthermore, history suggests that, even where the Arctic may not be a driver for conflict, it is still a potential theatre of operations.

As geographical and environmental change in the Arctic continues and the rate of retreat of seasonal sea ice becomes clearer, greater certainty will be brought to the Arctic. In the meantime, it should be noted that divisions caused by uncertainty are currently neither intractable nor unbridgeable. The Arctic remains a region where the vested parties broadly share common interests and goals: from the indigenous populations who seek greater development, balanced by protection of their culture and environment, to the Arctic and non-Arctic governments seeking further access to resources and trade. As such, the Arctic is currently a region of relatively low tension, but in order to remain this way its diplomacy must evolve as quickly as the sea ice retreats.

A zone of uncertainty

The areas of uncertainty in the Arctic are closely interrelated. They all stem from the vagueness of projections of environmental change in the region. The Arctic is clearly warming, and has been since the middle of the nineteenth century. The one certainty to be found in this is that warming will continue and is in fact accelerating, but the exact timing and trajectory is unknown.

This makes it difficult, if not impossible, to predict exactly how the region will develop politically and economically. Whether the Arctic will be a region of competition as states jockey for favourable positions and seek to maximise territorial claims is largely dependent on the economic viability of the High North. Yet the amount of potential resources that can be exploited is not yet clear: differing claims have confused the issue, while future markets for minerals and hydrocarbons may make the expense of extraction too great for profitable exploitation. Operating in the Arctic is already proving challenging for resource companies, and the barriers to exploitation – be they physical, economic, political, regulatory or cultural – are likely to remain.

Similarly, it is impossible to project the timing and degree to which Arctic maritime shipping routes will become globally significant and competitive with the present alternatives. That they will become more accessible is inevitable; that they will rival the Suez Canal is not. The future of shipping through the region depends not just on the retreat of sea ice, but also on the construction of infrastructure on the relevant coasts, the resolution of regulation and legal instruments for shipping, including the status of routes through Russian or Canadian territorial waters, and any ancillary costs, such as icebreaker leasing and transit fees. Even then, the routes will only be open seasonally for the foreseeable future.

The uncertainty over geography and economics also introduces uncertainty into politics and governance. It is unclear whether a multi-instrument governance and security architecture for the region will keep pace with change in the Arctic. The ability of the Arctic littoral states to cooperate among themselves and with the non-littoral states is also in question, given their differing perceptions of opportunity and threat in the region.

A zone of confrontation

While such uncertainty makes accurate prediction of the future of the Arctic impossible, a broader analysis of the strategic trends likely to affect the region is feasible.

One such trend is that the continuing change in the Arctic will mean wider interest in the region from extra-Arctic states, which will in turn affect the geopolitics of the region. Some Arctic states may react negatively to the perceived intrusion by outsiders, while others may welcome the investment and commercial interest. The increased interaction with non-Arctic states has the potential to sharpen divides among A5 and A8 states, or strengthen fault lines that already exist between, for instance, NATO and non-NATO countries. It is feasible, for example, that Moscow's eagerness to open up the NSR to traffic from China may sit uneasily with those European and North American states suspicious of Chinese diplomatic and military activity in the region. The possibility of Greenland's independence further complicates the Arctic geopolitical map, raising the possibility of an economically underdeveloped state with a small population and juvenile institutions interacting with some of the world's most powerful countries.

These shifting geopolitical positions create the possibility, although not the certainty, of diplomatic confrontation. This possibility is only furthered by the fact that no organised regional governance structure exists. The Arctic Council is an intergovernmental forum rather than an international organisation, so the current environment of cooperation is enforced purely through each government's current policies, rather than institutionalised through an organisation.

The probability of military confrontation is currently low, but the retreat of sea ice could force countries to address the disputes they have long harboured, perhaps exacerbating the resentment they cause in the short term. The A5 in particular have guaranteed the primacy of international maritime law; however, the rule of law requires not just statutes and structures but also effective dispute-resolution and enforcement mechanisms, and a readiness by all parties to use them and abide by the results. The indications are that this will be the case, with Canada, Denmark and Russia submitting their claims to the Commission on the Limits of the Continental Shelf, but until the findings have been adjudicated and the results accepted, full cooperation cannot be taken for granted.

Even if military confrontation is unlikely, the Arctic will continue to become a more strategic region for military forces, and politically cooperative processes could easily be undermined by aggressive military deployments. In particular, any further use of the Arctic for ballistic-missile defence would almost certainly foster mistrust, while unexplained and rapid deployments or procurements in the North would be viewed warily. The fact that security cooperation in the Arctic lags some two decades behind the political, economic and environmental cooperation exemplified by the Arctic Council only makes military mistrust more likely.

The lack of a security architecture, much like the lack of an institutionalised governance structure, means that there is no formal construct in which to embed the currently positive cooperative military–military trends. The Arctic could foster collaboration in the often antagonistic relationship between Russia and NATO, and arguably is already doing so, but its long-term effects may be diluted without the institutionalisation of this cooperation.

A zone of cooperation

Despite these slight risks in the Arctic, the overall environment and trends in the region are collaborative and peaceful. While states are naturally eager to further their own interests in the region, these are not being pursued in a purely zero-sum fashion that would be more redolent of the Cold War.

One of the main reasons for a lack of intense competition in the North is the fact that there are few disputes over ownership of resources themselves. Almost all potential resources are in undisputed territory, either on land or in EEZs. Even where there are overlapping claims, they are either benign, such as on Hans Island, or currently being handled through established international legal frameworks, such as those over the Lomonosov Ridge and extended continental shelves in the Arctic Ocean.

The potential for further political disagreements does exist, particularly over seabed minerals in the potentially overlapping continental-shelf claims or fishing beyond the EEZs, but these have yet to materialise owing to the lack of technical ability to exploit these resources and the difficulty in accessing still ice-bound areas of the ocean.

Littoral states also recognise the mutual benefit to be gained from the opening of the Arctic. This is the case not only for resource extraction – where the concept of mutual gain helped finalise the Russo-Norwegian Barents Sea agreement in 2010 after four decades of negotiation – but particularly in the maritime shipping industry. Shipping between Arctic ports, and bulk shipping from Arctic to non-Arctic destinations, especially of hydrocarbons, is likely to see the greatest and earliest increases. Russia currently stands to gain the most from more open shipping routes, from internal communications as much as from foreign trade, and hence Moscow is being directly encouraged to develop cross-border and multilateral relationships with a view to encouraging a safe and regulated shipping route through the NEP and especially the NSR. The fact that countries beyond the Arctic, particularly in Northeast Asia, also stand to benefit from these shipping routes should also encourage their positive engagement in the region.

While the Arctic is often viewed as an unexplored frontier, and there is much uncertainty over various aspects of the future of the region, it is not entirely a legal and governance vacuum. The Arctic Council is not a comprehensive governance model for the region, and it is unlikely to become an overarching organisation in the foreseeable future, but it is a pragmatic institution that helps foster collaboration. As the organisation and regional cooperation develop, the council may become a central pillar of a multi-level, multi-instrument regime. With better inter-state relations in general, fewer boundary disputes and a history of cooperation, the Arctic is a zone of relatively low tension and is better placed than many other parts of the world to develop stable governance structures.

The generally cooperative atmosphere in the Arctic has not yet been undermined by military competition. There has certainly been an increase in military activity as sea ice has retreated, but this is from a very low base and is far from the militarisation seen during the Cold War. For some of the military deployments and procurement, it is difficult to argue that they have a purely 'security' focus, given that they seem more suited to strategic or symmetric, conventional warfare, such as Russia's ballistic-missile submarines or Norway's advanced frigates and missile craft. Nonetheless, the overall growth in military capabilities has been relatively restrained in comparison to earlier periods, and driven more by the knowledge that the retreat of sea ice will create vast areas of water that will require governance, as increased traffic will demand security and safety.

The various militaries of the Arctic have, in fact, been more focused on cooperation and building nascent military–military relations than engaging in competitive procurement or gunboat diplomacy. Bilateral military–military meetings, joint exercises and Track 1 or Track 1.5 multilateral gatherings (involving, in the first instance, military personnel and, in the second, military personnel and civilians) have begun to foster a sense of collaboration and openness among the various militaries, and while at a nascent stage, it is being further encouraged by the only two agreements negotiated under the Arctic Council, which have prioritised maritime safety and security issues. Maintaining this momentum will be no easy task among countries that harbour deep suspicions and mistrust, and it could easily be hijacked by events elsewhere in the world that lead to a deterioration in collaborative endeavours. Nevertheless, the Arctic is a region where cooperation is more likely than it is elsewhere.

Similarly, in the field of law enforcement, non-military or paramilitary agencies could be useful tools in confidence building, particularly as it is theoretically easier to have constabulary or environmental agencies coordinate with one another than it is for militaries, given the level of wariness within and between militaries. Some coordination already occurs, albeit not in an Arctic-specific context, whether through the North Pacific Coast . Guard Forum or the North Atlantic Coast Guard Forum. This is only likely to increase, given the two Arctic Council agreements and the possibility of greater coordination on fishing in the high seas of the Arctic Ocean in the future.

Northern exposure

The stated aspiration of all the Arctic countries, as reflected in their Arctic strategies and documents, is to develop and maintain a region of peace, stability and prosperity. This helps explain why all states have come to focus on cooperation and collaboration, rather than zero-sum competition.

Such an approach is a strong base from which to develop regional collaboration, but it is not inevitable that a stable governance structure that can embed the current trends will be developed. The very thing that makes the Arctic a linchpin and bellwether of global environmental and geopolitical change is that the region's physical environment is far from stable, and that the changes in that environment will not be steady or linear.

Thus, policymakers are faced with a rapidly moving and intangible target, and managing the evolving strategic trends that emerge from these changes is a major challenge. How the level of shipping increases; how this will affect inter-, intra- and extra-Arctic relations; and how nations cope with greater numbers of vessels without having the constabulary capabilities in place, amid a desire to avoid antagonising other states, will prove to be a difficult test for countries in the region. Currently, with the various incentives in place for cooperation, the probability of militarisation and confrontation is low.

Simply by virtue of its ongoing shift from what was effectively a no-go zone to the world's newest neighbourhood, the Arctic provides opportunities for innovative and precedent-setting solutions and initiatives. If policymakers get it right, and avoid repeating the mistakes of the past, the Arctic could become a model for other parts of the world.

In this sense, there are key areas for improvement in regional relations. The first is simply in the gathering, collation and sharing of information. This was the original, and remains the principal, role of the Arctic Council, but it has been restricted to environmental and sustainable-development issues broadly construed. Cooperation would be maximised, and uncertainty minimised, if this function could be formalised, extended or strengthened, both for hard-security issues and for the soft-security activities of security-sector actors. For example, improved data collection and sharing on issues such as hydrography will enable better analysis of potential shipping routes, reduce the risk of serious accidents and reinforce mutual confidence. At the same time, operational information sharing, such as collaboration over Automatic Identification System data, would facilitate cross-border law enforcement and build confidence among the various states. Such cooperation need not necessarily be under the aegis of the Arctic Council – it could be pursued, for example, through a maritime-security working group created alongside the six existing groups. Nevertheless, from an organisational standpoint, the council offers an efficient pathway as an established institution.

The two existing treaties negotiated by the Arctic states, prompted by the Arctic Council – the search-and-rescue and oil-spill response agreements – have focused on issues of maritime safety, where constabulary and military forces will be particularly involved in implementation. This is a sensible first step to building confidence between otherwise suspicious armed services. Moving from maritime safety to maritime security, particularly in areas of joint concern, such as illegal migration and trafficking, would enable constabulary, and potentially military forces, to collaborate and diminish any lingering misgivings between them. This is an ambitious task, but steps towards such a goal could include a clearer separation of military and constabulary roles for services operating in the Arctic (as has been achieved with the maritime-safety agreements) and greater collaboration between the coastguards and maritime paramilitary forces that exist.

There is, of course, a great deal that needs to be done in terms of regulation and legislation concerning the increasing economic exploitation of the Arctic. This is in large part a matter for national legislatures – US ratification of UNCLOS or an updated Russian national law governing the NSR are two prominent examples. In areas that naturally transcend or cross borders, such as shipping and fishing in international waters, there is value in developing regulatory regimes on a collaborative (bilateral, multilateral or circumpolar) basis. Customs, excise and cargo inspections are of value to all countries, and will require some interaction between the relevant agencies and governments. Finally, unresolved issues of interpretation of aspects of UNCLOS need to be addressed. The Arctic states all accept UNCLOS as the overarching legal framework for Arctic waters, as do the most important non-Arctic stakeholders, as a condition of their observer status on the Arctic Council. Some issues are bilateral (the Russia–Norway boundary agreement, or disputes between Canada and Denmark, for example) and require little more than good will to resolve. But multilateral issues involving not just the Arctic littoral states but countries outside the region demand something more than an ad hoc approach.

These are all piecemeal factors that, when combined, can construct a web of interdependence and agreement that resembles a political and security architecture. Even without a formal regional organisation, such agreements can support the international forum that is the Arctic Council, which should remain the primary medium through which agreements are reached to minimise any sense of exclusion. This, therefore, reduces uncertainty over intentions, just as climate change clarifies the future accessibility of the region. These issues do not need to be tackled immediately, but without further regional interaction over the coming decade, there is a danger that diplomacy will lag behind the retreat of the sea ice.

Some levels of interaction may prove to be too ambitious, particularly in the area of military and paramilitary activity, but the motivation for further agreement and collaboration exists, and will likely encourage intra-Arctic discussions. A further motivation will be the fact that the region will never again be a sideshow. Soon – perhaps sooner than many suspect – the Arctic will take its place as a key part of the global system, and as one of many regions that require stable and effective governance for continued security and cooperation.

For all the talk of uncertainty in the region, it is clear that the sea ice will continue to retreat and the strategic importance of the Arctic will increase. Extra-regional interest and interference in the region will further complicate already developing intra-regional relations; economic exploitation will further expose the agenda of indigenous populations, local governments and international investors; and global trade and markets will be affected by this new frontier.

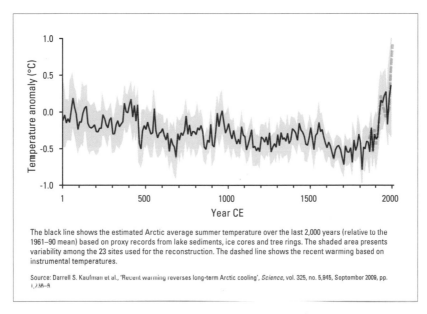

The black line shows the estimated Arctic average summer temperature over the last 2,000 years (relative to the 1961–90 mean) based on proxy records from lake sediments, ice cores and tree rings. The shaded area presents variability among the 23 sites used for the reconstruction. The dashed line shows the recent warming based on instrumental temperatures.

Source: Darrell S. Kaufman et al., 'Recent warming reverses long-term Arctic cooling', *Science*, vol. 325, no. 5,945, September 2009, pp. 1,236–9

Figure 1.1. **Changes in Arctic summer temperatures over the last 2,000 years**

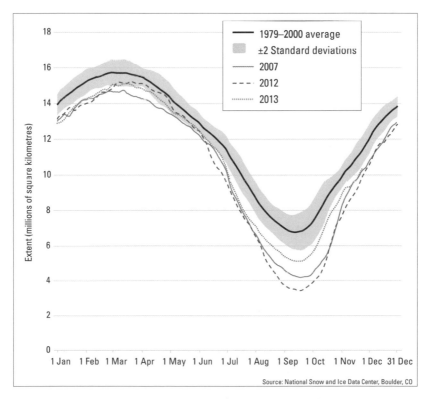

Source: National Snow and Ice Data Center, Boulder, CO

Figure 1.2. **Arctic sea-ice extent by month for 2007, 2012 and 2013**

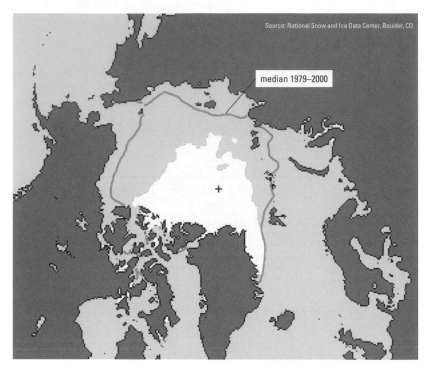

Figure 1.3. **Minimum Arctic sea-ice extent, 16 September 2012**

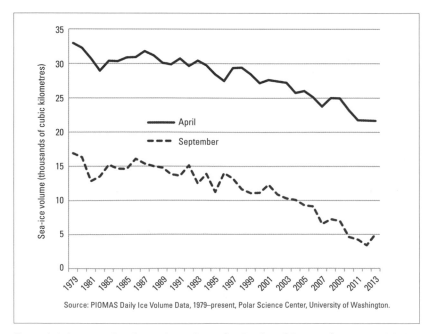

Figure 1.4. **Average Arctic sea-ice volume for April and September, 1979–2013**

Table 2.1 **Main producers and percentage of global production for non-petroleum minerals production in the Arctic, 2005**

Mineral	% of global production	Primary producers	Secondary producers	Minor producers
Palladium	40	Russia		
Diamonds (gem)	33	Russia, Canada		
Diamonds (ind)	21	Russia		
Platinum	15	Russia		
Apatite	11.4	Russia		
Cobalt	11	Russia		
Nickel	10.6	Russia		
Tungsten	9.2	Russia	Canada	
Zinc	7.8	US		Russia
Vermiculite	5.8	Russia		
Lead	5.6	US		Russia
Chromite	4.2			
Copper	3.8	Russia		Finland
Iron	3.6	Sweden	Russia	Norway, Finland
Silver	3.6	US	Russia, Sweden	Canada
Gold	3.2	Russia	US, Canada	Finland, Sweden
Coal	2.1	Russia		Norway, US
Bauxite	1.9	Russia		
Titanium	0.3			

Source: Solveig Glomsrød and Julie Aslaksen (eds), 'The Economy of the North 2006', *Statistics Analyses*, Statistics Norway, 2006, pp. 37–66.

Table 2.2 **Contribution of Arctic resource sectors to the regional and national economies of the Arctic states, 2005**

	Oil, gas and pipelines		Non-petroleum mining		Fishing and fish processing		Forestry, wood and paper		Arctic GRP	
	% GRP	% GDP	% GRP	% GDP	% GRP	% GDP	% GRP	% GDP	US$bn	% GDP
US	29%	0%	4%	0%	1%	0%	0%	0%	12,500.0	0%
Canada	8%	0%	20%	0%	0%	0%	0%	0%	1,080.00	0%
Finland	0%	0%	1%	0%	0%	0%	10%	1%	192.00	9%
Greenland	0%	0%	6%	6%	12%	12%	0%	0%	1.72	100%
Iceland	0%	0%	0%	0%	7%	7%	0%	0%	12.71	100%
Norway	0%	0%	0%	0%	7%	0%	1%	0%	289.00	6%
Faroes	21%	21%	0%	0%	0%	0%	0%	0%	1.51	100%
Russia	50%	6%	4%	1%	1%	0%	2%	0%	750.00	13%
Sweden	0%	0%	7%	0%	0%	0%	6%	0%	366.00	5%

Source: Glomsrød and Aslaksen (eds), 'The Economy of the North 2008', *Statistics Analyses*, Statistics Norway, November 2009, pp. 37–66. Currency conversion factors into US$ taken from IISS *The Military Balance 2006*.

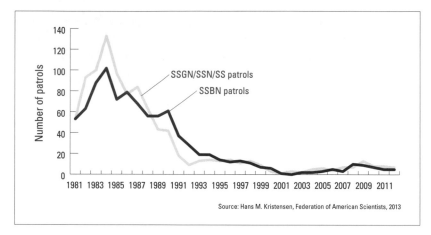

Figure 1.5. **Russian SSBN and general purpose submarine patrols 1981–2012**

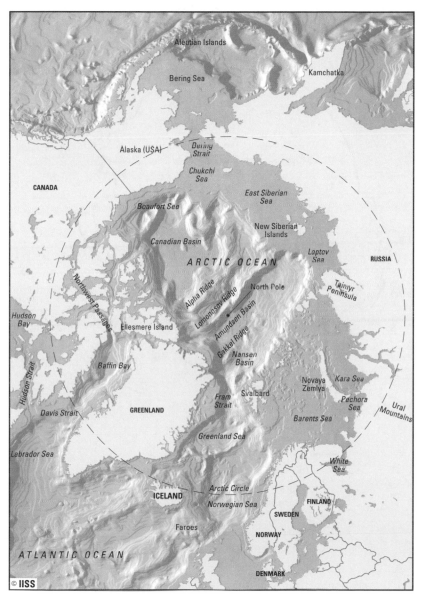

Map 1. **The Arctic Ocean and adjacent seas**

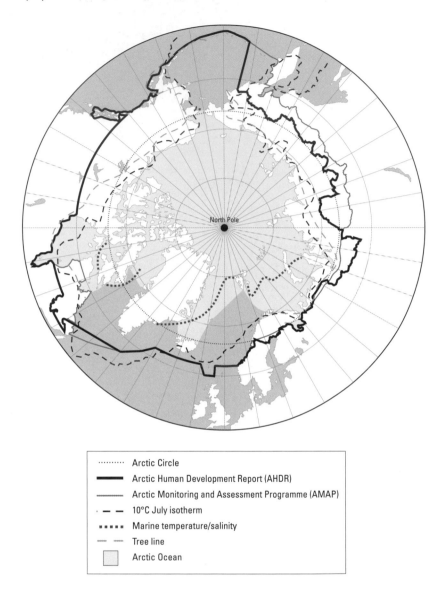

··········	Arctic Circle
——	Arctic Human Development Report (AHDR)
————	Arctic Monitoring and Assessment Programme (AMAP)
· — —	10°C July isotherm
▪▪▪▪▪	Marine temperature/salinity
— —	Tree line
▨	Arctic Ocean

Map 2. **Definitions of the Arctic**

Map 3. **Economic geography of the Arctic**

Adelphi books are published eight times a year by Routledge Journals, an imprint of Taylor & Francis, 4 Park Square, Milton Park, Abingdon, Oxfordshire OX14 4RN, UK.

A subscription to the institution print edition, ISSN 1944-5571, includes free access for any number of concurrent users across a local area network to the online edition, ISSN 1944-558X. Taylor & Francis has a flexible approach to subscriptions enabling us to match individual libraries' requirements. This journal is available via a traditional institutional subscription (either print with free online access, or online-only at a discount) or as part of the Strategic, Defence and Security Studies subject package or Strategic, Defence and Security Studies full text package. For more information on our sales packages please visit www.tandfonline.com/librarians_pricinginfo_journals.

2014 Annual Adelphi Subscription Rates			
Institution	£585	$1,028 USD	€865
Individual	£207	$353 USD	€282
Online only	£512	$899 USD	€758

Dollar rates apply to subscribers outside Europe. Euro rates apply to all subscribers in Europe except the UK and the Republic of Ireland where the pound sterling price applies. All subscriptions are payable in advance and all rates include postage. Journals are sent by air to the USA, Canada, Mexico, India, Japan and Australasia. Subscriptions are entered on an annual basis, i.e. January to December. Payment may be made by sterling cheque, dollar cheque, international money order, National Giro, or credit card (Amex, Visa, Mastercard).

For a complete and up-to-date guide to Taylor & Francis journals and books publishing programmes, and details of advertising in our journals, visit our website: http://www.tandfonline.com.

Ordering information:
USA/Canada: Taylor & Francis Inc., Journals Department, 325 Chestnut Street, 8th Floor, Philadelphia, PA 19106, USA. UK/Europe/Rest of World: Routledge Journals, T&F Customer Services, T&F Informa UK Ltd., Sheepen Place, Colchester, Essex, CO3 3LP, UK.

Advertising enquiries to:
USA/Canada: The Advertising Manager, Taylor & Francis Inc., 325 Chestnut Street, 8th Floor, Philadelphia, PA 19106, USA. Tel: +1 (800) 354 1420. Fax: +1 (215) 625 2940. UK/Europe/Rest of World: The Advertising Manager, Routledge Journals, Taylor & Francis, 4 Park Square, Milton Park, Abingdon, Oxfordshire OX14 4RN, UK. Tel: +44 (0) 20 7017 6000. Fax: +44 (0) 20 7017 6336.

The print edition of this journal is printed on ANSI conforming acid-free paper by Bell & Bain, Glasgow, UK.